Auguste Bartholdi (1834-1904)

True Light on
The Statue of Liberty
and its Creator

ANDRE GSCHAEDLER

LIVINGSTON PUBLISHING COMPANY
NARBERTH, PENNSYLVANIA

Dedication

As the Statue of Liberty originally was, this book is dedicated to Franco-American Friendship.

"Oui, cette belle oeuvre tend a ce que j'ai toujours aimé, appelé: la paix entre l'Amérique et la France—la France qui est l'Europe— ce gage de paix demeurera permanent. Il était bon que cela fût fait."

"Yes, this beautiful work aims at what I have always loved, called for: peace between America and France — France which is Europe — this pledge of peace will be permanent. It was a good thing that this should have been done."

VICTOR HUGO contemplating the
Statue of Liberty in Paris,
November 29, 1884

Preface

When I came to America for the first time I was not welcomed by Liberty raising her light "beside the golden door." I sailed into San Francisco Bay through the Golden Gate. I had my first view of the Statue of Liberty later. However, having been born and reared in Auguste Bartholdi's birth place I was familiar with the museum which used to be his house, and whenever I crossed a park I saw the monument of the sculptor standing next to an easel supporting a model of the Statue of Liberty. It was not my original intent to write a book about this topic as I took it for granted that everyone was familiar with the name of the creator of the monument which is today an American symbol. When I discovered that this was not the case I endeavored at every opportunity to revive the memory of an artist of whom my home town is proud. In the process I accumulated a mass of data and unearthed many facts which surprised me. This encouraged me to do further research making more discoveries until I had more than enough material to write this book.

André Gschaedler
December 18, 1965

vii

Acknowledgments

When research work for a book is spread over a period of many years, it is difficult to remember by name all the persons who have helped you. First of all, I wish to thank all the librarians — in the United States and in France — who have placed their collections at my disposal. I want, however, to thank particularly Mlle. Mollet. Thank you also for those who have written on the same topic in recent years and with whom I have corresponded. The one I am most grateful to is Mr. J. Betz. I also wish to thank Mr. P. E. Koenig, Mr. B. Levine and Mrs. W. Price.

On many instances I had to call upon the services of photographers, and in this respect Mr. Ohresser had been particularly helpful. A number of people at Liberty Island have given me valuable information. I like to remember Mr. S. Pickering, who had a small piece of the copper of the Statue of Liberty in its original color.

This book could not present such a large amount of new material if it were not for the help given by Mr. A. Husser. I should also like to acknowledge the support given me by newspaper editors and organization presidents who gave me opportunities to write or speak about my work while it was in progress. Foremost among them were Mr. J. Habert and Mr. A. Halm.

Once my manuscript was ready, it was thanks to Miss J. Cleavenger that it took its final form. English not being my native language, and this being my first book, a number of things had to be corrected. She did it without interfering with my style. Mr. L. Edwards' work on the index spared me a tedious task. Lastly, I want to acknowledge the help received from the Livingston Publishing Company, particularly from Mrs. K. Teigen and Miss F. Amadio in the preparation of the book for publication in accordance with my wishes.

As I am reaching the end of these acknowledgements I fully realize that many more people would deserve a word of thanks. I beg them to forgive me. I may be able to rectify omissions at a later date.

André Gschaedler
December 18, 1965

List of Illustrations

---

[1] Another copy was found at the *Conservatoire National des Arts et Métiers*, Paris. The firm Miege, Buhler and Co. owns at present the workshop where the Statue of Liberty was built.

[2] The ceremony was held in the courtyard of the *Musée Bartholdi*. The third person from the left in the first row of people standing in the background was Dr. Albert Schweitzer. On his right was Mr. Joseph Rey, mayor of Colmar. The white-haired gentleman in the foreground, wearing a coat and holding his hand on his back was the author's father who represented him at the commemoration. The speaker was Mr. Jacques Betz, author of a book entitled *Bartholdi*, published in French in 1954.

[3] Her features inspired Bartholdi's portrayal of Liberty (see page 79).

[4] The unfinished face of Liberty still has a hard look which did not pass unnoticed and which was to disappear later.

Contents

Contents

Prologue

The visitor of Colmar in Alsace, after seeing the main tourist attraction of the city, namely the Altar of Issenheim by Grünewald, may want to go sight-seeing. Walking leisurely through the narrow streets of the older part of the city, he may come to the square which surrounds St. Martin's Church, which the local people call the Cathedral. On the one side the houses are particularly picturesque; the main one has a Renaissance loggia carved out of yellow sandstone. The visitor may be curious to see what lies beyond a two-arched passageway on the right, which leads into Merchants Street and right in front of an imposing gateway, wide enough for the passage of horses and carriages and closed by a tall and massive two-paneled door, with a smaller entrance for everyday use. A sign on the right says *Musée Bartholdi* and gives the times when the museum is open to the public.

Few people visit the museum, except during the summer when there are many tourists in the city. Those who take the time to go inside the building are usually overwhelmed by the large number of interesting items. Visitors from the United States are surprised to come across so many reminders of their own country. How could it be otherwise! This was the birthplace and home of Auguste Bartholdi, creator of the Statue of Liberty.

As soon as the visitor steps into the inner courtyard of the house, he immediately feels that he is in an artist's home. A group of three figures supporting a globe stands in the middle of the paved yard. The first reminder of America is the statue of its discoverer, Christopher Columbus, on top of a pillar, carved by Bartholdi, which in its final form is in Barcelona, Spain. Inside the house all objects are placed as if they were in an inhabited home, and since visitors are able to go from one room to another and not restricted to looking through doorways, they are not allowed to wander around unaccompanied. Things might disappear. For many years, until January 1964, the visitors' guide was Monsieur Husser, who used to run an upholsterer's workshop in the yard of the museum. Whenever visitors came in, he left his work, collected the modest admission fee, and took them around individually or in small groups. He once told the author that if visitors were allowed to roam at will inside the building many more would come. Large groups used to be turned away because most of the rooms were, and still are, too small to hold many people at the same time while Monsieur Husser was giving his explanations. When he happened to be inside the building, Madame Husser, his wife, would lead the visitors to the floor where her husband was. When he was away Madame Husser conducted the tours herself. Thanks to this way of taking people around the wealth of the museum has been well preserved, and it is only recently that the municipality of Colmar "borrowed" some pieces of furniture. It is to be hoped that they will be returned in due course. Monsieur Husser was an elderly man, over eighty, but in the summer of 1962, when the author last saw him at the museum, he was still going up and down to the third floor of the building as many times as needed to show people around.

The house contains furnishings and works of art from two main origins, namely family heirlooms which have always been in Colmar, and furnishings which used to be in the Bartholdi home in Paris and were brought here after the death of the artist's widow. Everything was willed to the city of Colmar for a museum. This explains why there seems to be furnishings from two houses instead of one. There are a drawing room and a music room, which look alike; there are a library and a study, both with many books, and a room called an office, full of books too. The use of many of the rooms is not obvious, a number of them must have been originally bedrooms. At the present time there is only one room with bedroom furniture which is open to visitors. Two large rooms on the first floor, one of them rather spacious, are used at present for the display of the numerous models of Bartholdi's works.[1] There the visitors will see Lafayette from Union Square, New York, modeled in clay. They will also see

2

the model of Bartholdi's Washington and Lafayette monument. The original is in Paris and a replica is in New York. There also stands the elaborate Lafayette monument which Bartholdi had hoped to erect on Lafayette Square in Washington, D.C. There is an amazing number of statues of Liberty of various sizes in clay or terra-cotta. Which one was the first? Does the very first model still exist, and if so, is it in Colmar? This will probably remain a mystery forever.

On the second floor water colors of the Statue of Liberty hang on the walls, as well as framed letters and awards received by the artist, a number of them from the United States. In the drawing room, above a red-silk-covered sofa hangs in a golden frame a full-size portrait of Bartholdi's mother whose dignified features were to inspire her son's portrayal of Liberty. This portrait is by Ary Scheffer, one of Bartholdi's teachers. Nearby are portraits of the artist and his wife painted by Benner. On the third floor at the top of the staircase a large silver globe rests on an easel. It was received by the artist as a remembrance of the more than 121,000 Americans who contributed to the fund to erect the Pedestal of the Statue of Liberty. It was given to Bartholdi by Joseph Pulitzer, publisher of *The World,* the New York newspaper that helped to raise money for the Pedestal.

Bartholdi's library possesses books which are no longer easily obtainable in the United States such as an eight-volume report by the Director General of the Centennial Exhibition of Philadelphia in 1876. There are also many folios of drawings, prints, and photographs which would deserve a careful cataloguing. However, the position of curator of the *Musée Bartholdi* is now only a part-time and honorary one with little time to spare for this type of work. A clause in the Bartholdi will stipulated that it was to be held by a Protestant.[2] About one fifth of the population of Colmar adheres to this faith. It is probable that this clause was inserted following a wish of Auguste Bartholdi's mother. Thanks to Monsieur Husser's kindness, the writer of these pages was able to spend many days in Bartholdi's home, looking through the library, the study and other rooms; opening cabinets full of family papers and professional documents, including material on the Statue of Liberty which is probably not available elsewhere. He was able to go in some of the rooms not open to the public and to handle personal belongings, such as the uniform worn by Bartholdi during the Franco-Prussian War. This uniform is nearly one hundred years old now, but in spite of damages done by moths it is still wearable and gives an idea of the figure of the man who owned it. Also preserved are Bartholdi's violin, a very old Amati, his rosetta of Commander in the Order of the Legion of Honor, and a laurel wreath which he received on the occasion of the unveiling of his Lafayette statue in New York City. The preservation of many of these items, especially the ones related to the early part of the sculptor's life, was due to the care and love of his mother. Mother and son were very close. Madame Bartholdi kept a great many letters from her Auguste who sent her everything which might interest her. They were writing one another nearly every day — sometimes just a few lines — and Madame Bartholdi classified all the letters, year after year, month after month, in envelopes which she marked in this manner: "Letters from Auguste, April-June 1876." There are some gaps in the sequence, for instance when her son was with her or when she stayed with him in Paris. The author was able to look through these letters which, to his knowledge, have never been used in a book on the artist and his work. There are also rough copies of some of Madame Bartholdi's own letters to her son. She kept everything — telegrams, clippings from newspapers, and sometimes entire newspapers with articles about the Statue of Liberty and other works by her son, which he had enclosed in his letters or sent separately. Many of these came from the United States and would be very difficult to come by in any one place. All this material, as well as some other sources, throw a new light on the Statue of Liberty and its creator.

CHAPTER ONE

Auguste Bartholdi until the eve of the Franco-Prussian War

In spite of encyclopedias and other publications which say that Auguste Bartholdi was born on April 2, 1834, the correct date is August 2, 1834. This author would have been flattered if he had been born the same day of the month just a few blocks away from Bartholdi's birthplace. But accuracy should come first. It is probable that this incorrect date was repeated by writers without anyone bothering to go back to the source. The date August 2, 1834 is engraved on a plaque above the sculptor's home in Colmar, and it is No. 394-2 in the Register of Births kept in the Colmar City Hall among the entries for the month of August 1834.

The fact that Bartholdi was born in August and was called Frédéric-Auguste is a mere coincidence. His mother's name was Auguste-Charlotte, and his father's name was Jean-Charles.[1] The eldest son of the couple received the name of Charles from Jean-Charles and Charlotte, maybe also because the grandfather's name was Jean-Charles. When the second son was born there was the mother's first name still available, hence Auguste, and there were Frédérics on both sides of the family.

Concerning the artist's last name, Bartholdi, a few matters must be clarified. In the family papers the name is sometimes spelled with a "y" instead of an "i". It is probably not of Italian origin. It is of interest to note that a representative of the Swiss branch of the

Bartholdis, Mr. Albert Bartholdi, used to live in New Jersey where he died recently. This gentleman was interested in Americans of Swiss origin. Although Bartholdi was given the names of Frédéric-Auguste and is thus designated in printed material, the artist liked to be called Auguste. In Alsace it is not necessarily the first name which becomes the usual one. Bartholdi signed his letters. A. Bartholdi, and his mother used to called him Auguste in her letters. As a rule he engraved on the base of his monuments A. BARTHOLDI. His monogram was an A and a B entwined, and many of these of various sizes in copper are to be found in the drawers of his desk in Colmar. When he went to the Copyright Office in Washington, D.C., in 1876 to register his Statue of Liberty, he was probably asked about his initial, and he gave his name as "Augustus F. Bartholdi".[2] Therefore it is incorrect to call him Frédéric A. Bartholdi. It should be either Frédéric-Auguste Bartholdi or just Auguste Bartholdi, and this is what the author proposes to do in the following pages.

Auguste Bartholdi's father, Jean-Charles, was a French civil servant in Colmar. Judging from a large ledger of the Bartholdis' real estate, which can be seen in the former Bartholdi home, with well drawn maps and measurements, a substantial income must have come from fields, pastures, vineyards, and woods located around Colmar, which were worked by seasonal laborers or rented to farmers and market gardeners. There is no doubt that the family lived very comfortably. After Jean-Charles' death his widow was able to live in Paris with her two sons and provide for their education, thanks to a steady income from real estate and other sources.

Madame Bartholdi whose maiden name was Beysser had a great influence on the life of Auguste, the younger of her two sons. There was only a difference of three years between Auguste and Charles, so they grew up together. Charles was to precede his brother in the field of the fine arts. However, while Auguste rose to the pinnacle of fame, Charles' life was unfortunate. While he was in his early thirties he became mentally ill. In a fit he very nearly threw Auguste out of a moving railroad carriage as the latter was taking him to see a doctor. In one of his letters to his mother Auguste mentioned that whenever the train passed near that spot he remembered this incident.[3] When it was proved that Charles was incurable, he was deprived of his civil rights by a court decision in 1863. Before this

6

happened, however, he had signed three promissory notes representing a total value of 25,000 francs in favor of a resident of Colmar named Mark Dreyfus. When this man's sons and heirs demanded the payment of these notes, a protracted lawsuit followed. Documents show that Madame Bartholdi, who was acting as the guardian of her son, claimed through her lawyer that these notes were void, that her son's signature had been obtained by trickery, and that they constituted a theft because at that time, in 1862, Charles' mental illness had already manifested itself "to the highest degree."[4] The lawsuit revealed that Fanny Spire, born Dreyfus, the sister of the plaintiffs, who was separated from her husband, the latter still living, had had adulterous relations with Charles Bartholdi for a period of twelve years. There exists a thick file on these matters in a secret safe in the Bartholdi home. On the cover of the file are the words "Concerns a sad affair, to be burnt." It is probable that Charles would have liked to marry Fanny, after her separation from her husband, but on account of her belonging to another circle, being Jewish, and having been married he did not dare tell his mother about the affair. Such a situation prolonged over a period of years was largely responsible for his mental illness. His condition was sometimes referred to in Auguste's letters to his mother as general paralysis. He was suspicious of quacks who wanted to try to cure his brother as knowledge in that field was still rudimentary in those days. Charles spent the rest of his life — he was to die only the year before the unveiling of the Statue of Liberty — living near Paris, attended by a valet who tried to amuse him when he was crying too loud. Auguste went to see him now and then reporting to Madame Bartholdi that he was not sure his brother recognized him. Charles was spending most of his time playing with neckties or raking paper. Auguste was extremely sorry for the fate of his brother whom at one time he had wanted to emulate in the artistic field. He once wrote to his mother that he wanted the Colmar museum to have at least one painting by Charles — his painting representing Christ.[5] Madame Bartholdi tried to keep in touch with her older son. There is a rough copy of a letter in which she asked him whether he would not like to see her and begged him to write.[6]

The unfortunate experience with Charles, who was lost to her on account of his illness, brought Madame Bartholdi very close to her second son. She helped him a great deal with his career as an artist; he would never have gone as far as he did without her. Later on, when Madame Bartholdi's health began to fail, he was worried when away from home. After the unveiling of the Statue of Liberty, which he very nearly missed because of his mother's condition, Bartholdi cut short his stay in the United States to return to his mother's side. He returned to America only after her death a few years later.

Relatively little is known of Auguste Bartholdi's youth. After her husband's death, as pointed out previously, Madame Bartholdi settled in Paris with her two sons. The family usually came back to Colmar during the summer vacations. At school Auguste was an average student, but at an early age he showed an inclination for the fine arts. His mother preserved very carefully small heads of dogs which must have been one of her child's first attempts at modeling.[7]

Among the friends of the family was the painter Ary Scheffer, who had acquired some fame. There is a bronze statuette of Scheffer by Bartholdi in the music room of the *Musée Bartholdi* in Colmar, dated 1862, and Scheffer's portrait of the artist's mother has already been mentioned. He encouraged the youth to take up sculpture rather than painting, but Bartholdi never gave up painting and drawing altogether as is shown by a large number of water colors and drawings kept in Colmar. Besides the studio of Ary Scheffer Bartholdi visited the studios of other artists, including that of Etex who helped decorate the Arch of Triumph in Paris. He also came under the influence of the famous architect Viollet-le-Duc.

The great test for a French artist is the *Salon,* a yearly exhibition of works of art in Paris. Bartholdi was only nineteen years old when he presented his group *The Good Samaritan* at the Salon of 1853. From that time on Bartholdi was to be an exhibitor in nearly every *Salon.* In 1855 his main exhibit, a bronze statue of General Rapp, must have been considered too large to be put inside the rooms of the *Salon* in view of the obscurity of its creator. It was placed in front of the building on the *Avenue des Champs Elysées.* Naturally the Parisian press could not avoid mentioning it and referring to its colossal proportions.

General Rapp was a son of Colmar. A commemorative plaque indicates the house where he was born, and his heart is enshrined in the city's Protestant church. General Rapp served under Napoleon I. When the city first decided to erect a statue to Rapp in 1841, the name of Bartholdi would not have been considered. He was at that time only seven years old and was still modeling dogs' heads. But, as often happens when a monument has to be erected by the people, the fund-raising campaign lagged, and the artist originally selected for the project was unable to meet his commitments. Later in life Bartholdi also experienced the problem of facing the demands of metal founders asking for their money and threatening to sell or scrap his statues. But this time he was on the other side of the fence, and this was a marvellous opportunity for the budding artist. His model was accepted, the subscription was concluded successfully, and the statue was unveiled in Colmar in 1856, amidst great festivities, after Bartholdi's return from Egypt. This was the first of a series of monuments by Bartholdi in his home town of Colmar.

Most of Bartholdi's monuments went through a harrowing experience at the time of World War II when the Germans returned to Colmar. During the previous period of German rule (1871-1918) Bartholdi's monuments were left alone. Some of them were erected during this period and the German authorities did not object to a monument to Bartholdi in his home town after the artist's death in 1904. In 1940, however, the Germans who came back to Colmar were Nazis. They mistakenly thought that the war was won and that they were back in Alsace to stay. They wanted to eradicate anything which would remind the people of their ties with France. They believed that destroying Bartholdi's monuments would help achieve their purpose. Rapp's statue, standing in the middle of the city's largest square, was their first victim. While the general's bronze statue was lying on the ground prior to being broken up a boy succeeded, at the risk of his life, in unriveting the great soldier's sword during the night. That sword was passed from hand to hand until it finally reached unoccupied France. Now it is back in Colmar in the hand of the general who stands once again on top of his pedestal.

In 1856, Auguste Bartholdi took his first trip to Egypt. Several albums of drawings and early types of photographs have been preserved in his former home in Merchants Street. They show what Egypt looked like more than one hundred years ago. Some sections of that country have not changed much. Why did Bartholdi take

9

that trip to Egypt? One would rather expect that an artist would take a trip to Italy or to Greece. It so happened that a couple of his friends, one of them the painter Gérome, decided to go to Egypt and asked young Auguste to join them. He was probably interested in the adventurous aspect of the voyage and in the opportunity to see the gigantic statuary in the valley of the Nile. The French had become very interested in Egypt after Champollion's unlocking of the secret of the Rosetta Stone. The little group of friends traveled deep into Egypt and even crossed the Red Sea, landing in Aden. Bartholdi took another trip to Egypt for business purposes later on.

After his return to France Bartholdi continued to work on various projects. Some of them became works of art still to be seen today, while others remained at the model or blue print stage. In the one instance, the *Palais de Longchamps* in Marseilles, Bartholdi's plans were used by another and the artist was involved in a protracted lawsuit in order to gain recognition for his ideas. He was successful. It is not possible to mention all the works produced by Bartholdi between his first and his second voyage to Egypt which was followed by his first trip to the United States. On the occasion of the unveiling of his statue of Rapp, the ribbon of Knight in the Legion of Honor was pinned on the lapel of the twenty-two-year old artist while his proud mother was watching.

Among the Colmar monuments by Bartholdi of particular interest are his Bruat Fountain and his Little Wintner. The former, which was unveiled in Colmar in 1864, does not exist anymore in its original form. It was another victim of Nazi fury during World War II. Bartholdi had conceived it as a fountain representing the five parts of the world with Admiral Bruat, a native son of Colmar who served in the Pacific and in the Crimean War, as the central figure representing Europe. Bruat was in bronze while the other figures were in pink sandstone from the Vosges. Africa was represented by a muscular Negro. This statue had a definite influence on Dr. Albert Schweitzer's career. This humanitarian, who was born and reared near Colmar, wrote in his memoirs that when he was still a child the sad and thoughtful face of this Negro had directed his thoughts towards Africa. He added that later in his life whenever he passed through Colmar he stopped to contemplate this statue.

When the Nazis destroyed the fountain during their period of rule in Colmar, debris remained on the ground for some time and among them the head of the Negro which was intact. Some Colmar people were able to bribe the guards with cigarettes and other items hard to get in those days, and got broken pieces. Thus the Negro's head became the possession of the owner of a restaurant in Colmar. Dr. Albert Schweitzer had a cast of it in his study at Gunsbach, a few miles from Colmar. When the author visited him there a few years ago Dr. Schweitzer told him that he believed that a Negro from the Ivory Coast had served as Bartholdi's model. After the war while it was relatively easy to restore General Rapp on his conventional pedestal, the restoration of the Bruat Fountain offered a problem because of its many statues. It caused a controversy in Colmar because of the cost and labor involved in recreating Bartholdi's work. Finally, the bronze statue of Admiral Bruat, which was found undamaged, was placed on a new fountain with modern imitations of Bartholdi's statues of the continents.[8]

The Little Wintner, unveiled shortly before the Franco-Prussian War, represents a small boy drinking an endless flow of water, simulating wine, from a tiny barrel called *loyala* in the Alsatian dialect. Next to him sits a small dog. The Nazis left this monument undisturbed since it had no political significance. A replica of it, exactly the same size, is in the lobby of the Drexel Institute of Technology in Philadelphia, and it is customary for students to rub the boy's toe for good luck before examinations. The rubbing which has been going on for years has turned the toe a shining yellow while the rest of the statue has preserved its bronze color. It makes one think of the foot of Saint Peter's statue in Rome. The position of the Little Water Boy as they call him at Drexel is not as good as that of the original in Colmar which sits atop a fountain at the corner of a large building. It is impossible to reach the toe without getting wet.

The origins of the Statue of Liberty go back to the decade when Auguste Bartholdi was working on Bruat and the Little Wintner. According to the artist's own recollections he happened to be a guest at the home of Edouard de Laboulaye, a scholar and a friend of the United States, some time in 1865. In the course of the conversation the topic of gratitude between nations came up, and it was claimed that this feeling did not exist. Italy was given as an example. France had been instrumental in her liberation from Austrian rule and in her unification. Yet the keeping of French troops in Rome to protect the pope and prevent the Italians from taking over that city as their capital had embittered the relations between the two nations. Laboulaye was said to have remarked that this might be so in the case of Italy, but that it would never happen in the United States where the names of Lafayette and Rochambeau were still cherished. He also said: "If a monument were to be built in America as a memorial to their independence, I should think it very natural if it were built by united efforts, if it were a common work of both nations." This was how Laboulaye's words were reported by Bartholdi, quoting from memory about twenty years later.[9] Although plans for the monument as a common effort by people on both sides of the Atlantic Ocean were not made until much later the idea of the Statue of Liberty may be traced to this occasion. It is possible that at that time Bartholdi had already become interested in creating that international monument, and that he always kept the thought in the back of his mind while other projects were keeping him busy.

Of particular significance among Bartholdi's new endeavors was his plan for a lighthouse at the Suez Canal. This great gateway was a French enterprise which was supervised by Ferdinand de Lesseps. By an interesting coincidence the two men who were together in Egypt in 1869 came officially as delegates from France to the United States for the unveiling of the Statue of Liberty. Since the Suez Canal was about to be completed the khedive of Egypt was making plans to modernize and embellish his country. Engineers, architects, and artists from all over Europe, but particularly from France, were coming to the Nile Valley in search of contracts. Bartholdi, who had previously visited Egypt, figured that a monument of his of gigantic proportions at the entrance of the great international waterway would help him in his career as an artist. From his correspondence with his mother one learns that Bartholdi thought that the success of this project was to be something of a gamble. A drawing of the monument had been shown to Emperor Napoleon III and to Empress Eugénie. The latter, to whom Ferdinand de Lesseps was related, was to open officially the canal to navigation. All the artist could get, however, from their Imperial Majesties was good wishes. "If I do not succeed," he wrote to his mother, "I'll try something else."[10]

The young artist left for Egypt at the end of March 1869. When he arrived in Alexandria Ferdinand de Lesseps tried to cool down his zeal, but this was not enough to discourage the future creator of the world's tallest statue. Mr. Barrot, for whom he also had a letter of recommendation, was the first person who really welcomed him. Mr. Barrot knew Dr. Burguières who was close to the Egyptian ruler, and through him Bartholdi obtained an interview with Ismail Pasha. This took place April 8, and the artist related it in a letter to his mother dated April 15.[11] The kedhive received him in Ismaila. The interview was held in a room with a long sofa against the wall. Bartholdi showed Ismail Pasha his drawing of the monument and a small statuette. The Egyptian ruler remarked that he would prefer to see the light carried on top of the head of the statue as the local women carry their jugs of water and other burdens. In order not to indispose him the young artist replied that this would be easy to do, but he put in parentheses in his letter, "it would not look as good." The artist asked for permission to leave his drawing with the Egyptian ruler and to see him again on the occasion of his visit in Paris scheduled for two months later.

After this interview Bartholdi revisited some of the places he had seen during his previous trip. At the Pyramids he found the stone where he had engraved his monogram and the year 1856, below which he carved 1869. He wrote to his mother in Colmar that he could see a great many possibilities for work in Egypt should his project for the Suez Canal not succeed and that he was drawing sketches. In the meantime he continued making useful friendships, including that of an official of the khedive's entourage. He offered to repair the bust of the latter's father.

In his letters to his mother, who was constantly in his thoughts, Bartholdi wrote some beautiful descriptions of his voyage. "I am looking at the stars," he wrote, "trying to remember our astronomical studies. Then my mind wanders, and I think that I see you far away beyond the horizon."[12] Venice softly shining in the morning mist with the snowy Alps in the background made a strong impression on the artist.

On the homeward voyage Bartholdi helped a British officer as an interpreter and in exchange got some conversation lessons from him. It looked as if he wanted to get ready for a future trip to America.

After landing in Venice the sculptor stopped on the shores of Lake Maggiore to have a look at the statue of Saint Charles Borromeo, a sixteenth century archbishop of Milan. At that time this was one of the world's largest statues, and according to Bartholdi the first known example of a statue made out of copper *repoussé*, a very thin material worked with the hammer inside and outside, and supported by iron beams. His future Statue of Liberty was to be made of the same metal. In addition to his practicing his English with the British officer and his visiting the Borromeo monument to see what a copper statue looked like, there are other indications that Bartholdi was already thinking of the possibilities offered by America. In two letters written to his mother in December 1869, there were references to a mysterious American. In the first one Auguste apologized to his mother for not having written her the day before because he had been busy during the whole morning with "my American."[13] In the second letter, mailed a few days later, he said:

I do not talk to you about my American because I do not know what to say. I have founded much hope on this project; I ignore what will happen of it. I shall therefore be able to give you information on this subject only when the matter is either decided upon or buried.[14]

The matter was buried in 1869, yet "my American" and probably others must have been talking. Several years later, at the time when the Statue of Liberty was an object of praise and of criticism, Bartholdi had to defend himself against accusations of having used for his New York monument the project which could not be carried out in Egypt. In a small book written in support of the fund-raising campaign for the Pedestal of Liberty he wrote:

Now, I never executed anything for the Khedive, except the features of a female fellah. Besides everyone has seen the model of the Statue of Liberty made at Paris, and only evilly disposed persons are ignorant of what it has cost me. I have never answered these small cavillings, but I think that I ought to notice them on this occasion.[15]

14

In an interview given to a newspaper man and published under the headline "French sculptor nails a vicious falsehood once more" the artist was quite outspoken on this matter. Referring to an editorial in a New York newspaper Bartholdi mentioned the "old lie" and said that the story went back to his offer to make a lighthouse for the entrance to the Suez Canal. This was to be:

a colossal statue of an Egyptian female holding a light aloft. It was declined on account of the expense. At that time my Statue of Liberty did not exist, even in my imagination, and the only resemblance between the drawing that I submitted to the Khedive and the statue now in New York's beautiful harbor is that both hold a light aloft. Now, I ask you, sir, how is a sculptor to make a statue which is to serve the purpose of a lighthouse without making it hold the light in the air? Would they have me make the figure (whatever it might be) hiding the light under its petticoat not to say under a bushel?[16]

Bartholdi continued referring to that malicious New York newspaper which he does not name: "I never executed anything for the Khedive except a little sketch which remained in his palace." He concluded the interview in the following manner:

My Statue of Liberty was a pure work of love, costing me the sacrifice of ten years and of twenty thousand dollars — little perhaps for Americans, but a great deal for me. The Egyptian affair would have been purely a business transaction. I declare most emphatically, and I defy anyone in the world to contradict me, that the Statue of Liberty was ever offered to any other government.[17]

This was speaking very emphatically indeed. Yet, while looking through unclassified papers in the Bartholdi home in Colmar this author came across several pictures of this Egyptian statue — one had a note in Bartholdi's or his mother's handwriting (they were very similar) saying that it was the monument for Suez. This picture is reproduced in this book. There was also a watercolor by Bartholdi of that statue. On seeing this picture, anyone not familiar with the particular features of the statue in New York harbor, such as the tablet in the arm, would exclaim: "But this is Liberty Enlightening the World!"

Now, it may be asked why did Auguste Bartholdi never have this picture reproduced by a newspaper? Why did he only speak about the "little sketch" left in the Egyptian ruler's palace? In the newspaper there is no reference to the statuette shown to the khedive and which is mentioned in the artist's letter to his mother of April 15, 1869. Yet, this statue was seen in Bartholdi's Paris studio by the Alsatian painter Goutzwiller, who claimed that the resemblance between Liberty and the Egyptian statue was only superficial.[18] In the *Musée Bartholdi* there are a number of clay statuettes which are considered variations of the model for the Statue of Liberty. This author recently saw not only one but two of these statuettes with the date of 1869 engraved on the base.

There cannot be any doubt that the Statue of Liberty is a variation of an earlier project. Great artists have sometimes used the same model in several of their works. It is evident that a tremendous amount of effort lay between a drawing or a small model and a monument like the Statue of Liberty. It ought also to be remembered that Bartholdi, although he was not depending on his art for a living, was looking for opportunities to produce, to create. Statues and monuments are luxuries, and even in the great days of the Renaissance they were not in great demand. Bartholdi, as an artist, was looking forward to seeing his models become figures of bronze or stone to be seen by the public just as an architect wants to see his blue prints become solid walls of concrete or brick. In the case of important projects several people usually compete for the commission. Only one gets it while the others have been incurring the expense of making models or drawings. Who can blame the losers for trying to salvage for other projects some of the features which they conceived? Whoever visits the large hall of the *Musée Bartholdi* full of models realizes that quite a number of them did not go any further than the model stage, because of lack of funds or because someone else got the job. Besides the models which can be seen by the public, there are some which were damaged and lie in the attic of the old home. Among the commisions that Bartholdi did not get was that for the Lafayette Monument in Washington, D.C. This was to be one of Bartholdi's several disappointments after the unveiling of the Statue of Liberty.

The statue for the Suez Canal was supposed to be a lighthouse. Since the Egyptian government was not interested in it, another place for a lighthouse could be New York harbor — in a country where there was plenty of money. In an artist's life much work is derived from social connections. A casual remark about a portrait or a bust may lead to a commission for one who knows how to take advantage of opportunities. Laboulaye's remark about that monument in honor of American independence had not fallen on deaf ears with an enterprising artist standing or sitting nearby, and it may have been discussed right away. On account of the special character of his profession, Bartholdi, as will be seen on several occasions in this work, had learned to be a diplomat and to flatter people, regardless of what he might think of them privately. It appears, therefore, that he wanted the American people to continue to believe that the Statue of Liberty had been conceived only for them. In his book in support of the Pedestal Fund the sculptor referred to the deep impression New York harbor made on him when he saw it for the first time in 1871 and added:

If, then the form of the accomplished work is mine, to the Americans I owe the thought and the inspiration which gave it birth. I was conscious when I landed at New York that I had found the idea which my friends had hoped for.[19]

Shortly before the Franco-Prussian War Auguste Bartholdi nearly got married. This marriage project is shrouded in mystery. Among Madame Bartholdi's papers are two letters dated September 8 and 25, 1868, respectively, one of which expresses wishes for Mr. Bartholdi's happiness and the other thanks for the announcement about the engagement. Another letter dated October 13, addressed to Bartholdi by Edmond About, a French writer and newspaper man, congratulates the artist about his forthcoming marriage. This letter written from a place close to Saverne in Alsace said that About was sorry to have missed the opportunity of meeting "the beautiful and intelligent person who will be Madame Bartholdi, but that everyone admired her."[20] This author has not been able to come across the name of the person, but from a couple of letters from Auguste to his mother it is apparent that it was she who had tried to arrange a marriage for her son, who wrote:

If I let myself be carried along by the matrimonial current I am running great risks, and I would not like to be involved incautiously by you. I beg you therefore to be careful in what you say or do, because I reserve for myself all my freedom. I would prefer if you want to reconcile me with marriage that you made it possible for me to see and meet the person you have in mind instead of talking about marriage or making compromising overtures. [21]

This was in November 1869. The following month all marriage projects had been abandoned, and the artist did not hide his satisfaction to be, as he wrote, "out of the boiling pot." However, he did not exclude the possibility of a later marriage.

If I ever meet a person who could make me believe in the possibility of true happiness I would let myself be drawn in, but to think of marriage, to make a decision of that kind and to look for someone, to make the best of it, never.[22]

A few years later the artist met a woman with whom he fell in love, but when his mother thought he should get married he was not ready for it. The Franco-Prussian War, which broke out the following year and separated mother and son for a long period of time, prevented Madame Bartholdi from trying again to plan something for her Auguste's future. But, as will be seen, she kept hoping that some day he would meet the right person.

Auguste Bartholdi and the Franco-Prussian War. The Sculptor's First Visit to the United States

The Franco-Prussian War was to be a turning point in the life of Bartholdi, as in that of many other Alsatians. Their native province was now separated from the mother country. Existing narratives about the history of the Statue of Liberty ascribe much importance to the Franco-Prussian War and to the disorders which followed it in Paris on account of the Commune for Bartholdi's decision to go to the United States and try to get people interested in the Statue of Liberty project. These circumstances only confirmed him in plans made long before his trip. It has been pointed out that after his return from Egypt Bartholdi had some dealings with a mysterious American in Paris. Finding that negotiations for an important project could not be carried on from a distance, he decided that he himself would have to go to America. When he informed his mother of his decision, Madame Bartholdi grew very worried at the prospect of her beloved son crossing an ocean. When he had gone to Egypt on two occasions, she had not been unduly concerned because the trips had taken place on an inland sea. But now it was different. In a letter dated May 31, 1870, Bartholdi wrote that he belonged to a generation to whom a voyage to America did not seem any more dangerous than a trip to Bordeaux or to Corsica. The mother replied that she was sorry to have been misunderstood. She said that she was afraid that her Auguste might be disappointed again. She was thinking about the possibility of a recurrence of the failure in Egypt, and she wanted to spare this to her artist son. Madame Bartholdi, however, wrote that she wanted him "to follow your inclination."[1] Bartholdi's reply was dated June 2, 1870. He wrote:

Concerning the dream of America, I limited myself to point out a certain contradiction between the end and the beginning of your letter. I repeat it. This project is an excellent thing and I firmly believe in it; whatever I may do it would benefit me materially and I would make a beautiful voyage. HOWEVER! ! ! (underlined twice in the letter) if I do not have the certitude that you share absolutely my tranquility and my confidence, *I won't have any peace of mind.* I would not be able to do it, and it would cripple me, and therefore would be useless.

You see therefore that I present this project under a very clear form and very reassuring for you. All the more so since we have a year to think about it.[2]

It is unfortunate that the letter in which Bartholdi described his project in detail was not with the others. It is probable that Madame Bartholdi kept it separately, as she did for some special papers. There appears to be no doubt that the artist planned to sail to America one year after he wrote the letter, i.e. June 1871. Political events did not delay his departure. He sailed in June 1871.

During the Franco-Prussian War Bartholdi served in the French armed forces as an officer — first in his native Alsace, then in other parts of France. His red and blue uniform, as has been pointed out earlier, is still hanging in a closet in a part of his old home not open to the public. From letters which he sent to his mother, usually through Switzerland, it is possible to follow Bartholdi's journeys, although he did not tell everything to Madame Bartholdi in order not to worry her. On October 1, 1870, he left Colmar, on the 4th he was in Tours, on the 16th in Besancon, and so forth. He had the opportunity to work with Garibaldi, one of those Italians who had not forgotten Italy's debt to France. Bartholdi called him a "curious personality." From Tours, to which he had returned, he wrote to his mother:

I sometimes have satisfactions. I am helping when I can those who are suffering. I am providing for the needs of poor soldiers. The day before yesterday I was able to obtain mercy for an Italian that they were going to execute by shooting.[3]

In December Bartholdi was in Bordeaux to which the French government had withdrawn on account of the Prussians' advance. He informed his mother that he was communicating with Parisian friends by carrier pigeons. Madame Bartholdi, who had not forgotten her recent setback in regard to her proposed son's marriage, felt that this might be the time to reopen the question indirectly. In one of the rough copies of her letters to Auguste, which she often kept, she wrote that she hoped that while he was in Bordeaux he would make friends — that there were very good Protestant families in that city. Most likely she would have preferred her Auguste to choose a wife from these well-to-do circles instead of the one he married later.

While he was in Bordeaux Bartholdi was sent to pick up arms which came from the United States, and he heard of the demonstrations in favor of Prussia organized by German-Americans. It was pointed out to him, however, that Germans who had lived in America for a long time did not dislike France. Such conversations with people who had been in the United States must have impressed Bartholdi to a certain extent, since he mentioned them as part of influences which led to the erection of the Statue of Liberty in New York harbor.[4] No doubt he must have wondered whether American opinion as a whole was still friendly to a defeated France, since the success of his cherished project depended on this to a large extent. Laboulaye had expressed his firm conviction that an unshakable friendship existed between France and the United States. What did Laboulaye think now, Bartholdi wondered, about the monument he had casually mentioned five years ago, which had set the artist's mind working? Bartholdi would try to see as soon as possible the writer who was probably at his home near the city of Versailles, in an area still occupied by the Prussians besieging Paris.

The outcome of the Franco-Prussian War was unfortunate for France: Alsace-Lorraine was lost to her. Bartholdi's home town of Colmar was now in a foreign country. The artist's beloved mother was there, safe but very worried. At first Bartholdi could not cross the border, since in the early days of German domination trips to

Alsace were subject to all sorts of restrictions. Thousands of people from Alsace-Lorraine left their homes, selling them for what they could get for them rather than live under German rule. It would have been expected that the Bartholdi family would do likewise. Auguste had been brought up in Paris; he had an apartment there and a studio. Madame Bartholdi had lived in Paris for many years while her sons were being educated, and she had a circle of friends whom she visited when she went to see her son. Leaving Alsace for good would certainly be easier for them than for the many thousands who did not have such good connections on the other side of the Vosges. Although they disliked German rule in Alsace, the Bartholdis never cut off all ties with the lost province. There must have been several reasons for this attitude — reasons of a material and of a sentimental nature. The Bartholdi family had a great deal of real estate in and around Colmar, as was mentioned earlier in this work. Much of this was in gardens, vineyards, and fields which could not be sold in a short time without incurring very heavy losses. The new masters of Alsace had set a time limit for those who wanted to leave for winding up their businesses and selling their homes and lands. By that time Madame Bartholdi was no longer young. She had never worked to earn her living, and had been accustomed to live comfortably from her income. This steady income had also greatly helped her son in his artistic career. The prospect of a loss of status and of a struggle to make a living was not very pleasant, so she decided to put up with the invaders, some of whom were billeted in her vast home for a while. There was also the sentimental side. As many Alsatians Bartholdi hoped that sooner or later France would recover the lost territory. He did not live long enough to see this happen. Also there were the artist's first monuments — Rapp and Bruat — in Colmar, actually the most important monuments he had conceived thus far. In great contrast to the Germans who came back in 1940, those of 1871 did not touch any of Bartholdi's monuments. They did not object to the city authorities looking after them and to the erection of other monuments by Colmar's native son. It has been seen what the 1940 Germans did. . .

Bartholdi finally succeeded in reaching Colmar via Switzerland in the spring of 1871. He stayed there a short time — just long enough to see his mother and settle some matters before resuming his plans to go to the United States. He needed to make sure that he would not be short of money while abroad.

Bartholdi left Colmar for Paris on May 27.[5] From Paris he sent letters to his mother describing the damage done by bombardments. She preserved pictures of Vavin Street, where her son lived, showing some gutted houses. Fortunately nothing happened to Bartholdi's studio. In June the artist wrote that he was having passport troubles. No wonder he had such troubles — 1871 was not a year for tourism! He also said that before making final arrangements he had gone to see Laboulaye who gave him letters of recommendation for friends in the United States. It is probable that Laboulaye or his connections also helped the artist in getting his passport. Laboulaye strongly encouraged Bartholdi to go to the United States and to propose to:

Our friends over there to make with us a monument, a common work, in remembrance of the ancient friendship of France and the United States... If you will find a happy idea, a plan that will excite public enthusiasm, we are convinced that it will be successful on both continents, and we will do a work that will have far-reaching moral effect.[6]

On June 21, 1871, Bartholdi landed in New York from a steamship of the *Compagnie Générale Transatlantique*. He spent about five months in the United States, traveling from coast to coast, meeting people for whom he had letters of recommendation, making new friends, and getting people interested in his project for a monument to Franco-American friendship. He had opportunities to meet such famous men as President Ulysses S. Grant, Longfellow, the poet, and Brigham Young, the Mormon leader. In spite of the many contacts Bartholdi was able to make while he traveled through the United States, the artist found out, as he wrote in one of his letters, that one of the main obstacles to his project was the American character that is "hardly open to things of imagination."[7] In another letter he remarked that one has to put up with quite a bit of annoyance on the part of those same people who will be enthusiastic if the project succeeds. There exists, or existed, a diary in which Bartholdi had put information about his doings while in America, but the author has been unable to trace it thus far and has had to rely on other sources. A passenger approaching New York by sea today looks at large masses of stone; in 1871 the artist was pleased to see grass after a long stay in the "realm of the fish." The coming and going of ferryboats in the port impressed him and their shapes reminded him a little of the floating bathhouses on the Seine in Paris. "In the distance one sees New York between Brooklyn and Jersey City. It looks as if they were one city, and in fact they make up one ensemble."[8] The artist added that they had separate city governments and compared them to the mystery of the Trinity.

Bartholdi's steamer docked at a North River pier. After getting through the customs he hired a carriage which took him to his hotel. In a very vivid manner he wrote down his first impressions of New York City. He described it as a milling of people in a hurry, some neglected streets, lamp posts of unequal heights, displays of goods on the sidewalks, booths as one sees them at fairs, uneven pavement, and so forth. He added that almost all the streets looked like this except the main streets which were usually well kept and lined with tall houses. Some of the things seen by Bartholdi are still part of New York's life in some districts. The better houses, he wrote, have flights of steps with porticoes and tiny lawns on each side. The artist's eye saw there a mixture of styles which he jokingly called: "*anglo-marseillais-dorico-chineso-badensis*."[9] The "badensis" at the end referred to Baden in Germany which is on the other side of the Rhine facing Alsace, and which from an Alsatian's viewpoint for a long time had been synonymous of bad taste.

Naturally as soon as he had found his bearings he sent a cable to his mother in Colmar, who was worried as long as her Auguste was at sea. She got it the very next day and excitedly replied:

I must admit that I was following you as in a dream. What an agreeable surprise to receive the marvellous and fairy-like dispatch! One feels like kneeling before him who has invented such a magical thing.[10]

Bartholdi kept his mother informed of all his doings while in the United States. She saved her son's letters, as well as the cables, postcards, pictures, and drawings that he enclosed in his letters. The artist was not as yet a figure for the American press, therefore this correspondence did not include newspaper clippings about receptions, unveilings, and other public affairs. He also wrote to Laboulaye. With the help of all this material, this author was able to follow the artist during his stay in America. Bartholdi's main purpose in crossing the Atlantic was to get support for his project and the more people he could meet the better. As usually happens in cases like that, quite a number of people whom he met were not of very much help to him. Moreover, arriving in New York early in the summer, Bartholdi found out that many of Laboulaye's friends and correspondents had already left the city.

Among the people whom Bartholdi met were Horace Greeley, editor of the *New York Tribune,* and William George Curtis who published *Harper's Weekly. Harper's* was frequently to publish pictures of Bartholdi's works. However, in 1871 these publishers listened with more or less attention to the Frenchman's plan for a statue. At that time none of them was inclined to give it much publicity. Joseph Pulitzer, who was to be the most ardent and efficient supporter of the Statue of Liberty project through a campaign for the Pedestal, became the owner and publisher of *The World* only twelve years after Bartholdi's first visit to the United States. Since the artist's proposed monument involved a large outlay of money the sponsorship of the rich would be useful. On his first trip to America Bartholdi met some wealthy people such as Cyrus Field, who had put a cable under the Atlantic. This project was bringing in good returns, while the usefulness of a statue of Liberty as a lighthouse was not too obvious. New York harbor had enjoyed prosperity without it for a long time. The sculptor also met Peter Cooper, a rich man. Yet, at this time America's wealthy people were not particularly interested in the Statue of Liberty, although a number of them did show up and were anxious to be seen at the unveiling ceremony fifteen years later. During his campaign to raise money for the Pedestal, Joseph Pulitzer taunted the Vanderbilts, the Goulds, and other rich people of the day for their lack of response to his appeals for contributions. Maybe they felt that the embodiment of Liberty in New York harbor would not be in the best of their interests.

Through his friends Bartholdi was introduced to various clubs in New York, such as the Lotos Club, which sponsored a great reception for him several years later when he had become famous. In 1871 he was just a visitor from abroad. He was also taken to the New York Club and to the *Cercle de l'Harmonie.* It appears that the matter of a Lafayette statue was discussed there. This project materialized in 1876, during the artist's second visit to the United States.

as a gift of the French government with the French residents of New York providing the pedestal. Bartholdi's stay in New York was an opportunity for him to renew his former friendship with John LaFarge whom he had met in Paris. The LaFarge family became Bartholdi's best friends. He often stayed in their home on Sunny-side Place in Newport, Rhode Island, and it was through them that he met his future wife. While in New York Bartholdi also thought of a site for his statue, and Bedloe's Island appeared to him the most suitable. In his later correspondence he often called it "Liberty Island," as it is called today. The selection of Bedloe's Island for the Statue of Liberty, however, was only made later on, following a survey and study by General Sherman whose devastating march through Georgia has left many sad memories. About a month after his arrival in the United States Bartholdi wrote:

Today, after a little sketching for projects, I went to the harbor to visit the island which will serve as a base for the monument, and which is in a situation admirably suited to what I want to execute. Unfortunately there is a fort and consequently a conflict with the army, but I think this will be solved after the work has received approval. That is the question. I believe that this undertaking will take very great proportions, and, if things turn out the way I think, this work of sculpture will take a very great moral significance.[11]

Bartholdi obtained a letter of introduction to President Ulysses S. Grant, who was residing at the time in the summer White House in Long Branch, New Jersey. The French artist was surprised at the unpretentious two-floor frame house close to the sea without any trees nearby, and at the "bourgeois" way of life of the President of the United States. He sat with the President on the porch. Grant was later to pay a visit to the Statue of Liberty under construction in Paris and to praise Bartholdi's work very highly. In the summer of 1871, however, although he listened with attention to the French-man's plan, he did not put any of his influence behind the project. It is known from other sources that Grant did not particularly like France. As a former victorious general he may have looked down on a country that had just suffered military defeat. Bartholdi wrote that he was a reserved man "like most Americans." The interview lasted about half-an-hour, but long enough for Bartholdi to notice many

26

little things such as the president's gouty father-in-law sitting next to a spittoon.

Bartholdi had also introductions to people in Philadelphia, Washington, and Boston. It seems that he took the Philadelphia trip soon after his arrival in New York. There he met Colonel John W. Forney, publisher of *The Press*. He was to have more to do with Forney later on, when the colonel came to Europe in 1875, as general commissary in Europe for the Philadelphia Centennial Exhibition. In this capacity he attended the banquet at the *Grand Hôtel du Louvre* in Paris on November 6, 1875, when the fund-raising campaign for the Statue of Liberty was launched. Forney even gave a speech on that occasion. In 1876 during the Centennial Exhibition, Bartholdi spent much time in Philadelphia visiting with the Forneys and making new friends.

Auguste Bartholdi went to Washington early in July 1871. He was there on July 4, and he was not favorably impressed by the Nation's capital. He thought that the cupola on the Capitol Building was imperfect, that the Washington Monument — which was only seventy feet above the ground at that time — would not be nice to look at, but that the intention of the project — with stones from all the states — was "poetic." From his letter Madame Bartholdi must have gained the impression that Washington in July was a city with "much dust, many Negroes, badly paved or unpaved streets, much sun, and lots of flies."[12] This was the first impression, but it is probable that the artist cared less about such things after his meeting with Senator Charles Sumner from Massachusetts. On July 15 he wrote to Laboulaye that the senator had received him very cordially and had done all he could to make his Washington stay very pleasant. Senator Sumner was a good friend of Laboulaye, whom he had visited in France. The senator had brought from France objects which decorated his home and Bartholdi must have felt immediately at home there. Sumner liked to entertain guests of foreign origin and Bartholdi may have met some. He had been a leading abolitionist, and his fiery attacks against Senator Butler of South Carolina had once caused the latter's nephew to hit him with a cane at his desk on the Senate floor. In 1871, however, Senator Sumner no longer had the influence he once had; he no longer was chairman of the Foreign Relations Committee. He died three years later. As a friend of

France, Sumner was naturally interested in Bartholdi's idea and he suggested he should return to Washington when Congress was in session.

All this traveling and visiting involved expenses, but the artist seems to have been well provided for. On July 13 he wrote to his mother in Colmar that she should not worry. She was particularly pleased when a letter from him reached her on August 2, the sculptor's birthday, a day when she was particularly thinking about her Auguste.[13] Later during the same month she wrote him about a letter of credit and entreated him to stay all the time needed for "your magnificent project."[14] Bartholdi visited Boston a number of times and was commissioned to decorate the tower of a church there, but the matter was finally settled only on the very last day of his stay in the United States. The artist hoped that this would repay him for his expenses during the trip, but he had some disappointments in regard to this project. While in Boston he used his letter of introduction to a friend of Laboulaye to obtain an interview with the poet Henry Longfellow, who was then residing at his summer home on the seashore. The poet whom Bartholdi called "The Lamartine of America" said that he was hoping that the artist's idea of a colossus on Bedloe's Island would arouse enthusiasm among "New Yorkers." The poet asked him to stay for lunch and the sculptor wrote: "I stayed with him, smoking a cigar, on his porch looking at the sun setting on the sea between small islands."[15] He added that when they parted the writer clasped his hand as if he had wanted to transmit electrically this pressure to his friends in France. Bartholdi was so charmed with the elderly gentleman that he went to see him again.

Since there was nothing more he could do in the East until the fall Bartholdi set out in August on his trip through the United States. He went all the way to California. He did not visit any place south of Washington, D.C., except for Alexandria. The South was still in the process of recovering from the Civil War, and he was advised to stay out of it. Among Bartholdi's papers in his old home in Colmar there are four railroad maps — Erie, Kansas Pacific, Central Pacific and Union Pacific. On the Erie railroad map he marked for his mother all the places he had visited, connecting them with a red line which showed his trip to the West as well as the places in the East where he went several times. The line connects Alexandria, Washington, D.C., Philadelphia, New York, Newport (Rhode Island), and Boston. From Boston it leads into Connecticut, touching West-field, Hartford, and New Haven and ends in New York. From there the line leads to Niagara Falls, then through Canada to Detroit and Chicago. The other railroad maps have no red line. However, letters, postcards, and photographs give a fair idea of where the sculptor stopped on his trip from Chicago to San Francisco and on the way back from the West Coast.

On August 12 Bartholdi stopped at Niagara Falls and had Samuel J. Mason of Point View, on the American side of the Falls, take a photo of himself next to an unidentified friend. The Falls are in the background. Bartholdi traveled to Niagara Falls amidst great honors fifteen years later shortly after the unveiling of the Statue of Liberty; crowds gathered at railroad stations to greet him and his party. He sent his mother a postcard from Chicago showing the Schermann Hotel, Clark Street, north of the City Hall. Bartholdi felt that Chicago was the most American city he had ever seen. He wrote that in 1804 the place had only five inhabitants, while in 1871 there were 299,000, 126 churches, and about 100 newspapers. Smoke darkened the sky. One saw an enormous population running around, pressed by the "stomach ache of business." One cannot understand, he continued, how all this could have come into being in such a short time. "It is marvellous." He added, however, that he would not like to have to live in such a city. What it lacked was charm and taste. Bartholdi also left us a vivid description of the West:

At a short distance from Omaha starts the Prairie. We traveled through it for about 800 kilometres. It becomes wilder and wilder as one approaches the Rocky Mountains until it finally looks like a desert. The Prairie starts becoming monotonous after thirty-six hours of traveling. In spite of this one can find a certain charm in this immensity which is like the sea. Now and again there is an unexpected sight such as a flock of antelopes or a town of prairie dogs. In the middle of these expanses one comes from time to time across a railroad station with a small cluster of houses. This is a town. Sometimes there are even a church and a hotel, but there are very few of them. However, I saw there crinoline frames, signs of progress which are testimonies similar to the carcasses of oxen which are often lying about on the old trail of the migrants. This old trail is only indicated by a few dusty ruts. It is like a large path — it is the track painfully made on the soil by countless migrants who dragged themselves for months in those vast expanses.[16]

The French traveler was greatly impressed at the sight of the Rockies which he approached in daylight. He used highly descriptive terms to describe them:

At the entrance to these mountains there are sights of extraordinary savageness. Only the savages are missing. Red masses of rock extravagantly shaped, burnt terrains, grey grass, red moss, no trees, dried up torrents — this is how the approaches to the mountains look. . . There are some diabolical sights as in fairy tales.[17]

Bartholdi made a stop at Salt Lake City and mailed from there two postcards to his mother in Colmar. One showed the Mormon Temple and the other Brigham Young's house. At Salt Lake City the sculptor was astonished to see well-dressed women walking next to filthy miners on dusty and caved-in streets. The Frenchman had an opportunity of meeting the great Mormon religious leader and "the happy husband of sixteen wives and the father of forty-nine children." Brigham Young would have liked to have had a portrait of himself painted by Bartholdi, but the latter declined and proceeded on his trip. Although Bartholdi was first of all a sculptor, he did quite a bit of painting in his spare moments. However, he seemed to have preferred drawing to painting. Many of his letters have drawings in them. One of them shows the railroad station in Washington, D.C., with a sign saying: "Look out for the locomotive." As far as painting was concerned he was not particularly keen about portrait painting, and that was probably one of the reasons why he did not care to stay in Salt Lake City for several days in order to paint a portrait of Brigham Young. He also probably figured that this would not help the Statue of Liberty project because the Mormons were not particularly wealthy in those days. Bartholdi preferred landscape painting to portrait painting. At the Centennial Exhibition in Philadelphia he exhibited two large landscapes with a few personages. One is called "Old California," and the other "New California." Both hang on the wall in the *Musée Bartholdi* in Colmar, as a memory of Bartholdi's visit to the West Coast of the United States in 1871.

The artist did not have much to say about his crossing of the plateaus, but he was greatly impressed by the descent into California. "One enters valleys and gorges, one passes through trenches and tunnels from one ravine to the other, skirting enormous masses of rocks. Some of the sights are magnificent."[18] About San Francisco he wrote: "I believe that for the time being the population's education is not of a high moral level. There are always ambitions and greeds. There is hardly room for anything else."[19] He thought, however, that this Babel was interesting to see and to study. He sent his mother a postcard showing Vernal Falls, Mirror Lake, and Yosemite Falls. He must have seen some, if not all, of these sights. In one of his letters he referred to a day in a stagecoach on a dusty road between Stockton and Sequoia Park. He therefore visited some of the landmarks of California which tourists still go to see today.

In all of the cities that he visited Bartholdi had tried to organize committees and correspondents for his great project. He probably did not find in the West too many people interested in contributing to the erection of a statue of Liberty in New York harbor as they had more immediate concerns. He did not stay in California very long. On his return trip he passed through Denver, Colorado. He wrote that this town, only twelve years old, already had ten barbers and three music dealers. The artist crossed once again the Prairie. There were still many buffaloes roaming around in those days. Bartholdi saw a herd about one thousand strong in the distance, but a few animals could be seen close to the railroad tracks. He noticed one of them watching the train go by from the top of a mound, standing against the sky, and looking like a large black-maned lion. He observed his traveling companions on the train, for instance the women wearing piles of false hair. Here and there one finds remarks about Americans in general. He thought that they lacked individualism, that the individual was obliged to conform and lived like "a drop of water in a torrent." He felt that Americans had no time to live. He noticed Americans' desire for bigness. "Everything is big here, even the *petits pois* (green peas)," he once wrote. However, this was one more reason for him to hope that his colossal statue would appeal to these people. The artist felt that probably one of the best sides of America was the interest in education. Also, he was greatly impressed by America's technical achievements, such as the tremendous bridges spanning abysses, tunnels under rivers, and so forth.

On the way back to the East Bartholdi stopped in Saint Louis and in Cincinnati. The sculptor was charmed by the thick forests through which the train traveled. They were beginning to take the shades of fall and had hardly been desecrated by the axe. He was back in Washington for the opening of Congress and made some new contacts. Yet, everywhere he heard that the initiative for his statue would have to be taken by the French, so Bartholdi decided to sail back to his home country and see what could be done there. Although his first trip to the United States had not given the hoped-for results, it had been far from useless, and it is probable that without it the Statue of Liberty would never have risen in New York harbor.

The balance sheet of this first trip to the United States may be summed up as follows: Bartholdi had made some friends who were to support him later on; he could now visualize where the Statue of Liberty would probably stand in the bay, and this was to be a help while working on it; he had got an order for a sculptural frieze on the romanesque tower of a Unitarian church in Boston. He had got that commission through a friend of the architect who was later to design the Pedestal for the Statue of Liberty. Bartholdi was to work on this project while in Paris. It is still to be seen high up on the church which is now the First Baptist Church in Boston. There is at each corner of the tower an angelic trumpeter, while on the sides are large sculptured groups representing four main occasions in the life of a Christian: baptism, first communion, marriage, and death. Some of the figures modeled by Bartholdi were reminiscent of some of the people whom he had met or whom he admired, such as the poet Longfellow. He also left behind a bust of Laboulaye. In a letter dated December 16, and written from Paris, he said that he thought that he was going to sell the bust.[20] It was eventually bought and presented to the Union League Club in Philadelphia. Later on it passed into private hands. Recently it unexpectedly showed up again in New York, and will probably be placed in the American Museum of Immigration which has been built close to the Statue of Liberty.[21]

CHAPTER THREE

The Beginning of the French Fund-Raising Campaign for the Statue of Liberty and Bartholdi's Second Trip to the United States

The five years which elapsed between Auguste Bartholdi's return to France in the fall of 1871 and his second trip to the United States in 1876 were to be very active ones indeed. In his Paris studio the artist worked on his project for the Boston church as well as on a number of other monuments. Some of these were cast and delivered during this period of time — one of them being his monument of Vauban, the great French fortifications builder of the seventeenth century. Others were only exhibited in one of the yearly *Salons;* several remained in the sculptor's studio waiting for the finishing touch. Bartholdi also continued working on the Statue of Liberty project and made a number of models for it. But most important of all, the fund-raising campaign got a good start during these five years and Liberty's arm in its final form could be shipped to the United States for public exhibition: first at the Centennial Exhibition in Philadelphia, and later in New York. In the original plan of Laboulaye and Bartholdi the whole statue was to be ready by 1876, for the hundredth anniversary celebration of the Declaration of Independence of the United States. But another ten years were to pass before it could be unveiled in New York harbor.

One of Bartholdi's first concerns after his return from the United States was naturally to see Laboulaye and to talk with him about the results of his visit in America. They were not able to meet until

December 3, 1871, when they had dinner together. That same month of December, there appeared in a Parisian newspaper an article of which Madame Bartholdi was very proud. The clipped article was put by her in an envelope on which she wrote: *A bien conserver* (To be saved carefully).[1] She certainly had reasons to be proud of its contents. It was No. IV in a series of articles on Alsace by the French author and journalist Edmond About, who had visited Colmar and the Bartholdi home while the artist was away in the New World. Edmond About went into much detail about his reception by Madame Bartholdi. The writer was entertained not in the old family home on Merchants Street but in a smaller house owned by the family on the outskirts of Colmar in a beautiful park along the river Lauch. That house was near a cottage, restored recently, still to be seen in the park which has so many ivy-covered old trees and so much undergrowth that it reminds one of a small forest. It is smaller now than it used to be on account of the construction of a street behind the house (Bartholdi Street). The city of Colmar has expanded and the park, which is privately owned, is now fairly close to the center of the city. People like to watch from a bridge the lordly swans which glide on the peaceful river. It is possible that Madame Bartholdi did not want to receive Mr. About in the larger house because the Prussians were still occupying some of the rooms or because most of the family heirlooms had been taken from there while the house was being occupied by strangers and had not been put back. Edmond About admired the ancestors' portraits — all denoting solid bourgeois qualities — and the many family antiques. Madame Bartholdi kept talking about her Auguste, and showed letters that she had received from him. She explained that during the Franco-Prussian War, in order not to worry her, he had made her believe that he was working in an office while he was at the front line. The proud mother showed the writer some of her son's works, and Edmond About was particularly impressed by a model of a monument which is still to be seen in the Colmar cemetery on the tomb of a member of the local national guard who had served under Bartholdi and had died in the defense of Colmar against the Prussian advance. The Voulminot monument shows the slab of a grave being lifted up by the bronze arm of a warrior making a desperate effort to seize again his sword lying slightly out of his reach. This monument symbolized the hopes of many people in Alsace-Lorraine that some day they would again be able to fight to regain their liberty from Germany. At that time it was doubtful that such a controversial monument could ever be put in the cemetery. Yet, it was unveiled on November 2, 1872. Alsace-Lorraine had become a territory belonging in common to all the states of the German Empire, reconstituted under Prussian leadership. Flushed with victory the Germans could afford to be tolerant. Of course, this was not to be always so. During World War I the monument became a place where people who were hoping for the return of Alsace to France would gather, and the Germans removed it. This author's uncle was arrested when he protested this removal. Later the Voulminot monument was put back in the cemetery, but in 1940, when the Nazis started destroying Bartholdi's monuments, it was taken away again. The monument is back in the Colmar cemetery, and the great improvement in Franco-German relations since World War II induces one to hope that the grave will not be interfered with again.

Edmond About's article was read by many people and even caused envy on the part of some members of the family in Paris who had kept away from Madame Bartholdi and her two sons while they were in Paris. Once the political situation was stabilized, it was again possible to travel between Paris and Colmar, and Madame Bartholdi spent the end of the winter and the early part of the spring of 1872-1873 with her son. Naturally there are no letters for this period of time. Auguste came to Colmar now and then, at least once a year, and helped his mother run the family finances and real estate. In 1874 mother and son took a trip together to Italy, bringing back beautiful memories to be cherished for years.

During the hard times that France went through as a result of the Franco-Prussian War, the city of New York, particularly its French residents, most of whom used to live in the area around Greenwich Village, did a great deal to alleviate the sufferings of the French people. In recognition of this generous help, and probably influenced by some of Bartholdi's friends, because the matter had been touched upon while the artist was in New York, Mr. Thiers, who was governing France during the period of recovery, commissioned Bartholdi to make a monument of Lafayette to be presented to New York. Bartholdi's Lafayette was exhibited at the *Salon* of 1873, where, according to a letter received in Colmar from Charles Blanc, a friend of the family, the statue "looked very fine."[2] This statue was to be unveiled three years later in Union Square, New York, where it still stands. This unveiling, which was Bartholdi's first great success in the New World, will be dealt with in due course. At the *Salon* of the following year Bartholdi exhibited the reliefs he had made for the Boston church, and they were shipped to America when the *Salon* was over.

At the time of the Franco-Prussian War the city of Belfort in the southwestern corner of Alsace had valiantly sustained a siege by the Prussians, refusing to surrender. On account of this stubborn resistance France was allowed to keep Belfort and the area around it, although she lost the remainder of Alsace under the terms of the Treaty of Frankfurt. In 1871 the city council of Belfort, wanting to commemorate the valiant stand of the defenders of the city by a suitable monument, opened a competition. Bartholdi's Alsatian heart was immediately enlisted, and he conceived one of his most striking monuments. It was a gigantic lion, wounded but still defiant, leaning against a mass of rock, holding a broken spear under his paw, and roaring to his enemies. A picture of this monument appeared in an illustrated magazine in 1874,[3] but it was unveiled only in 1880 because the funds needed for it could not be obtained as rapidly as was anticipated. Bartholdi's "Lion of Belfort" is his most famous monument in Europe, but it was never to acquire the widespread symbolic meaning that the Statue of Liberty has.

The year 1874 saw the beginning of Bartholdi's dream of erecting Liberty in New York harbor. A committee called the *Union Franco-Américaine* was founded to implement the project with Laboulaye as its president. The plan was announced through the press that same year. However, the project did not really get started until the following year. Among Bartholdi's papers is a menu for a banquet held on September 6, 1875. No less than ten courses are listed, one of which was *Homard à la Yankee* (Lobster Yankee Style).[4] However, the great banquet which launched the fund-raising campaign was held two months later on November 6, and received much publicity through the press. On September 28, 1875, an appeal from the *Union Franco-Américaine* appeared in the French newspapers. Its main passages were as follows:

The great event which is to be celebrated on the 4th of July, 1876, allows us to celebrate with our American brothers the old and strong friendship which for a long time has united the two peoples.

The New World is preparing to give extraordinary splendor to that festival. Friends of the United States have thought that the genius of France ought to display itself in a dazzling form. A French artist has embodied that thought in a plan worthy of its object, and which is approved by all; he has come to an understanding with our friends in America, and has prepared all the means for executing the plan.

It is proposed to erect, as a memorial of the glorious anniversary, an exceptional monument. In the midst of the harbor of New York, upon an islet which belongs to the Union of the States, in front of Long Island, where was poured out the first blood for independence, a colossal statue would rear its head.

We will in this way declare by an imperishable memorial the friendship that the blood spilled by our fathers sealed of old between the two nations.[5]

This appeal was signed by Laboulaye and others whose names were to remind readers of America's relationship with France, such as Lafayette, Rochambeau, and Tocqueville. Everyone was asked to contribute his or her mite. Since the Statue of Liberty was to be a joint undertaking by France and the United States, the American public had to be informed. A letter from Laboulaye appeared in the *New York Tribune,* dated Paris, October 15, in which the French writer said that France desired to participate in the Centennial of American Independence and wished to celebrate with the United States "that noble liberty which represents the glory of the United States, and which enlightens the modern people by its example."[6]

The banquet of November 6, already referred to, took place at the *Grand Hôtel du Louvre* in Paris. There were two hundred guests, including the descendants of Lafayette and Rochambeau who had signed the appeal. The menu included fourteen courses. Glowing praises of the American Revolution and of Franco-American friendship were heard. The banquet hall was decorated with French and American flags and portraits of Presidents MacMahon and Grant. Dominating the end of the hall was a floodlit painting of the Statue of Liberty shining at night in New York harbor — a reminder of the purpose of the banquet which was to open officially the subscription for the monument in France. The American press as well as the French press, headed by Edmond About, was well represented.

Among the American speakers were Washburne, the American minister in Paris, and Colonel Forney, who had come for the Philadelphia Centennial Exhibition which he represented in France. Naturally, the main speaker on the French side was Laboulaye who recalled Franklin and Lafayette. It was announced through the press that contributions would be banked at the *Société Générale,* 54 Provence Street, Paris.[7]

On November 25 Bartholdi wrote his first letter to his mother on stationary with the letterhead of the Committee of the *Union Franco-Américaine,* 175 Saint Honoré Street, Paris. In the center of the upper part of the sheet are the following words: "Subscription for the erection of a commemorative monument for the hundredth anniversary of the independence of the United States."[8] The *Union* was therefore ready for business. Reactions to the project, as reported in the press, varied from unbounded enthusiasm to vicious criticism. One man asked for the privilege of donating the metal for the Statue; an American resident of Paris gave a large amount and said that the roles should be reversed and that a statue should be placed on the banks of the Seine. He promised ten thousand dollars, a large amount in those days, if someone would start the project. This took place later. There is now a Statue of Liberty, one quarter the size of the New York one on a bridge of the Seine. More about this in due course. Someone else suggested that the Americans meet the French half-way and subscribe an equal amount as the French. On the other hand there is a clipping from an unnamed United States newspaper in the Ford Collection on the Statue of Liberty, in the New York Public Library, without any date, but going back probably to 1875, which threw cold water on the enthusiasm of the French and their American friends. This article said that the French did not know the topography of the harbor, otherwise they would not say that the light would be visible far at sea. The correspondent wrote that it would only light dilapidated wharfs, and he suggested that a more satisfactory place would be the Battery because people wanting to scribble their names on the Statue's legs would not have to cross over to the island to do so. According to the article the Statue's light would facilitate the work of counterfeit ticket agents and others who prey on immigrants. It continued in that tone, also suggesting Coney Island, an amusement area, as a suitable location for the Statue of Liberty. This is an example of the bad taste of some of the articles which appeared now and again in the American press about the future Statue and hampered the raising of money on this side of the Atlantic. Fortunately, there were also a number of people in America who supported the project right at the beginning. *Harper's Weekly*, for instance, while stating that it was unlikely that the Statue would be ready the following year, added that the appeal should not be made in vain.[9]

The year ended as the fund-raising campaign in France was gaining momentum through collections, benefit performances, and other means, Nothing, however, had been started in America. On March 14 Bartholdi wrote to his mother that he had visited the musician Gounod who was going to compose a Liberty cantata for the forthcoming benefit evening at the Paris Grand Opera. A few days later the sculptor informed his mother that he was about to ship his great fountain to Philadelphia and that he thought that it would be a success at the Centennial Exhibition. About six weeks later Bartholdi was to take his second trip to the United States.

The great benefit performance at the Opera took place on April 25, 1876. Laboulaye made a grand fund-raising speech. He outlined the situation in France and in America at the time of the American Revolution. He continued by saying that to celebrate the hundredth anniversary of Franco-American cooperation a symbol was needed and was being looked for:

when a gifted artist, an artist who is dear to us, one of the sons of Alsace who remained French, Mr. Bartholdi, had the idea for this monument which is portrayed at the back of the hall (cheers in the audience). This Liberty will not be the one wearing a red bonnet on her head, a pike in her hand, who walks on corpses. It will be the American Liberty who does not hold an incendiary torch, but a beacon which enlightens.[10]

Laboulaye concluded his speech with these sentences which crystallized his thinking:

May this statue, a monument to an old friendship, weather time and storms! One century from now America, with an enormous population, will celebrate its second centennial. She will have forgotten us, but she will not have forgotten either Washington or Lafayette. This Statue of Liberty, created in a common effort, will preserve these precious memories which are the links between the two nations; it will preserve among future generations, like a sacred tradition, the eternal friendship of the United States and France.[11]

Later in the evening Gounod's cantata was performed. It started with this sentence: "I have triumphed! I am one hundred years old! My name is Liberty!"

On May 6, 1876 Bartholdi left for the United States with the French delegation to the Centennial Exhibition. This was naturally a good opportunity for him to present anew to the American friends of France his Statue of Liberty project. This second stay in the United States was to be his longest, as he did not leave until January 27, 1877. This was the turning point in the history of the Statue of Liberty. At the time of his departure from France the fund-raising campaign was well under way, but nothing to speak of had been started in the United States. When he left the country a committee had been formed to start raising money for the Pedestal of the Statue.[12] Also, this second voyage placed his name before the American public — his Lafayette statue was unveiled in New York amidst great fanfare; he had several exhibits at Philadelphia and received some awards. There also occurred a change in his private life. He came to America in 1876 a bachelor, and left in 1877 a married man.

During his trip across the ocean to the United States Bartholdi enlivened the long hours on board the ship by drawing colored caricatures of the members of the French delegation to the Centennial, with humourous comments under each picture. These cartoons were published in the form of a booklet after the sculptor's return to France.[13]

On May 18 the French group arrived in Philadelphia, and Bartholdi must have been very proud to see his monumental fountain occupying the center of the quadrangle between the Main Exhibition Building and the Machinery Building — a choice position. This fountain was later to be placed in Washington, D.C. The French sculptor, however, was expecting a more significant example of his art — the arm holding the torch of Liberty. He hoped that this would arouse the interest of the American people. The arrival of "my arm," as he used to say, was delayed over and over again.

The American press was starting to pay more attention to the project. A newspaper in New York published a picture of the plaster cast of the hand of the Statue holding the torch. An article stated that the Statue of Liberty with its Pedestal would be 220 feet high. Actually with its Pedestal it was to be a little over 300 feet. The article added that the Statue would not be cast in bronze, but in copper *repoussé,* and this was correct.[14] The American public had to wait another ten years to see the Statue of Liberty completed, but this was a beginning. As time went on the press gave the public correct and incorrect information about the forthcoming Statue. Much of this was collected by clipping agencies, mainly the *Argus,* and mailed to Bartholdi. The author has been able to use this collection which is kept in the *Conservatoire National des Arts et Métiers* in Paris.[15]

While in Philadelphia Bartholdi was not missing any of the shows. He wrote to his mother that he was mailing to her separately a newspaper with an article on "the great statue," and another showing pictures of a parade of shriners through the city's streets. He added that the city was always decked with flags on account of the parades and that the night before there was a parade of Roman Catholic Germans with banners and a band. He thought that Americans were funny people to indulge in such parades in uniforms. "They have a craze for banners and parades," he wrote. He was wondering in view of all this what July 4 would be if they started that early with the parading.[16] In Philadelphia Bartholdi stayed on Walnut Street; then he went on to live on Livingston Place with the Aubert family. General Tyndale was also his host during one of his stays. He often complained in his letters about the summer heat, saying that he took several cool showers a day. During the heat waves he once wrote: "I live like a Moslem — that is I do everything at a slow pace."[17] While the artist was in Philadelphia he did quite a bit of traveling to other cities to visit friends and to foster his Statue of Liberty plan. In June he spoke at the Offenbach Supper for artists at the Hotel Brunswick on Fifth Avenue, between 26th and 27th Streets, in New York, trying to get support from this group. According to a reporter, on that occasion he showed that he was a master at the skill of Demosthenes as well as that of Phidias.[18] New York artists and American artists in general, however, remained rather cool to the project. Maybe some of them were envious of Bartholdi and felt that he already had had too much success since his Lafayette statue was in New York at that time. Bartholdi went to see the Lafayette in Central Park, near 65th Street, where it had found a temporary location. Accompanying him was his friend Henri de Stucklé, an engineer of French origin, who worked for the New York waterworks and welcomed Bartholdi as his house guest whenever the latter stopped in New York for a few days. Stucklé was to build a pedestal for Lafayette. A correspondent of the *Courrier des Etats-Unis*, New York's French newspaper, who went to see the statue wrote that it "has much more movement than could be noticed on the photograph of the original model." He added: "This is really Lafayette, aged 19, animated by the ardor of youth and fired by the noble passion for liberty."[19] On July 4 the sculptor had the satisfaction of seeing a large lit-up picture of the Statue of Liberty on the New York Club Building in Madison Square. This display had been set up by his friend Stucklé.[20] A few days later the *New York Tribune* printed an article on "France's Monumental Gift."[21] Auguste Bartholdi was no longer a foreign visitor, known only to a few people, as he had been in 1871, and the image of his Statue of Liberty was becoming gradually familiar to the public.

By the middle of July 1876 Bartholdi was back in Philadelphia. In a letter to his mother dated July 14, France's national holiday, he explained that the members of the French delegation were packing to return to France. Most of them, including Bartholdi, had been on a committee set up to judge exhibits at the Centennial Exhibition so that prizes and awards could be given. The artist added that he would have to stay in the United States because "I'll receive my wretched arm only on August 1."[22] He expected that he would have to stay until September 6, date of the unveiling of his Lafayette in New York. The prospect of this ceremony, which was to be a great success for him, and would have been for many artists an occasion to look forward to, was but a minor concern in Bartholdi's mind. Had he not attended many unveilings, starting with that of his General Rapp in Colmar when he was only twenty-two years old? His main interest was the Statue of Liberty. His reputation and self-respect were at stake. If he failed as he wrote to his mother in the letter of July 14: "I would look like a ridiculous day dreamer and an inefficient man." He felt that the display of Liberty's arm in Philadelphia would be a significant step toward his goal, but its arrival was delayed several times. Worrying about the arm and the

42

prospects of the Statue itself made Bartholdi quite sick at one time, as will be seen later.

A further disappointment came to him in July when he traveled to Boston and saw that the tower of the church was not ready for his sculptures. He also found out in Boston, as in New York, that many of the people who had befriended him in 1871 were out of town for the summer. Meanwhile the artist was getting more publicity. A newspaper published an article in New York about the expected arrival of the arm, about Bartholdi's fountain on the Centennial grounds, and his friezes for the Boston church. The paper also said that his health had not been good on account of the heat, but that it had improved while he was in Newport. Then, visualizing the Statue of Liberty in its future setting, the writer of the article continued:

standing upon the threshold of New York, which is the doorway of the Union, she will seem to offer the freedom of the New World to the thousands who flock to us from the Old. Type of that freedom which gathers the downtrodden and oppressed to her bosom, even as a hen gathers her chicken under her wings, she will appear to invite them to a continent where the last slave has ceased to exist; where all climates enrich and diversify the soil and all peoples assimilate; where all religions erect their several altars to the universal God and millions worship dissimilarly in friendship.[23]

A haven for the tired artist was always the LaFarge home in Newport. The French sculptor went there on a number of occasions, usually spending several days in order to find relief from the city's heat and from his worries. His August 1876 stay in Newport was probably his longest. The LaFarge house on Sunnyside Place had a long porch where it was nice to sit. Also John LaFarge had a small studio, and Bartholdi sat down to paint a large canvas with New York harbor and the Statue of Liberty. Father LaFarge, S. J., John's son, recalled the artist's stay in his autobiography.[24] He was kind enough to authorize this author to look through the family papers now deposited in the New York Historical Society Library, but there was little of interest about the relationship between Bartholdi and his LaFarge friends. There may be more to be uncovered somewhere else. Much time was spent in the evening talking on the porch. The beach was nearby, and the artist enclosed in one of his letters a small painting to show his mother what that beach looked like.[25] Mrs. LaFarge was very kind to him. "She is the best soul you can imagine. I had met her only once formerly."[26] The understanding lady must have often tried to dissipate her guest's worries with kind words while he was impatiently waiting for the arrival of the arm and torch of the Statue of Liberty. August 1 had passed without its showing up. Madame Bartholdi in Colmar was sharing her son's anxieties, and she made sure that he got a cable with greetings on his birthday, August 2.

September was to be a month of great excitement for the artist. Liberty's arm arrived at last! An article in *The Press,* dated September 1, described the arm as being located on the shore of an artificial lake near the Thomas Cook and Co. Building and the *New York Tribune* Building, very close to Machinery Hall. This was a good place, and it had been kept free for the monument in spite of the long delay in shipping. The paper stated that the whole piece — it included the torch, the hand and part of the forearm — was thirty feet high. It added that if New York did not provide the money for the erection of the Statue, Philadelphia certainly would, and the Statue of Liberty would rise on George's Hill or Lemon Hill in Fairmount Park, awaiting the next Centennial.[27] This started a rivalry between Philadelphia and New York for the possession of the Statue which was to last until all the money necessary for the Pedestal was finally raised. One of the attractions at the Centennial Exhibition was the balcony around the torch of the Statue on which ten to twelve people could stand at one time. Today, visitors to the Statue of Liberty are not allowed to walk beyond the interior of the head. Bartholdi had not waited for the arrival of the arm to have the whole Statue copyrighted. At the end of August, accompanied by his friend Henri de Stucklé, the sculptor called at the Copyright Office in Washington, D.C., and duly registered his work, describing it as "Statue of American Independence." The application which was entered under No. 9939 of 1876 was accompanied by photographs of a drawing of the Statue of Liberty and of a model. That number 9939, together with the date of August 31, appears on some of the small reproductions of the Statue of Liberty which exist in various locations.[28] The sculptor was disappointed later when it proved to be very hard to control reproduction of the Statue of Liberty. It would probably have been better in some respects for the Statue's shape if it had been possible to do this, since some of the ones sold as souvenirs of a visit in New York would have horrified Bartholdi. On the other hand the widespread popularization of Liberty has helped her to become very well known in the United States and abroad as a great symbol to the point that most people do not know that it was originally devised as a commemorative monument of France's participation in the War for American Independence and as a strengthening of Franco-American friendship.

About the middle of September 1876, Madame Bartholdi in her Colmar home received a letter from her son dated New York, September 7. Enclosed was a laurel leaf from the wreath received by her Auguste at the unveiling of his Lafayette statue in Union Square, New York, and a flower from a bouquet which he had received on the same occasion. The leaf and the flower have yellowed the paper in which they were sent. Bartholdi wrote that he was sorry that his dear mother could not have been there for the unveiling, and that he had been asked to speak both in French and in English. "This is only the beginning," the sculptor added, "I must stay until results have been obtained for *the other*."[29] By this he meant, of course, Liberty. After the letter Madame Bartholdi received newspapers from the United States with entire articles about the unveiling, many clippings, and a couple of photographs of that ceremony. On one of these the artist marked in red the place where he had been standing during the ceremony so that his mother could visualize the whole affair. Madame Bartholdi kept all these souvenirs with great pride. Actually, she kept more material on Lafayette than on Liberty, maybe because she got more or because it was her son's first unveiling in America. It must also be said that when the Statue of Liberty was unveiled, ten years later, she was ill and unable to arrange things the way she used to previously. All these souvenirs helped Madame Bartholdi to bear her long separation from her son. Auguste had never been away for such a long time, not even during the Franco-Prussian War. She had to be patient if she wanted him to reach his supreme goal, and she always made sure that he would not be short of funds.

The unveiling of Bartholdi's statue of Lafayette was an occasion the residents of Union Square and many New Yorkers who saw it were to remember for a long time. In some respects it gave Bartholdi a foretaste of what was to happen ten years later at the unveiling of Liberty. The Lafayette statue, it will be recalled, was a gift of the French government, while money for the pedestal was provided by the French residents of New York City. The monument shows the young French officer about to land from a ship holding his sword against his heart. The inscriptions on the pedestal read: in front, "Lafayette"; on the one side, "To the City of New York, France in remembrance of sympathy in time of trial, 1870-71"; on the other side, "As soon as I heard of American Independence my Heart was enlisted, 1776"; in the rear, "Erected 1876." On the day of the unveiling the statue was wrapped in a United States flag connected by a cord with a flagstaff erected right behind the monument. The statue was to be unveiled by pulling that cord and hoisting the flag to the top of the staff. On each side of the monument rose two poles with French flags. The ceremony was preceded by a parade of troops and civic organizations, carrying signs, including a number of French societies, such as *L'Union Alsacienne* of New York which still exists today. The unveiling started at 4 P.M. in the presence of a distinguished audience, most of them sheltered by umbrellas. There was the usual speech-making as Mr. Edmond Breuil, consul-general of France in New York, presented the statue in his country's name and Mayor William H. Wickham accepted it in the name of the city. Among the descriptions of the unveiling the author found none more striking than that given by a reporter in *The Irish World*. Bartholdi must have been particularly pleased with it because he mailed the whole newspaper to his mother; all of the speeches are given in full. There are also lengthy biographies of Bartholdi and of Lafayette. The hoisting of the United States flag took place immediately after the mayor's acceptance speech. The reporter wrote:

At this point M. Bartholdi, the sculptor, unveiled the statue, and then ensued an indescribable scene. A great cheer went up from the multitude in the square and in the surrounding buildings. All bands present played the *Marseillaise* and the cannon thundered forth in a salute, while the telegraph wires signaled the waiting artillerymen in the harbor to join in paying tribute to Lafayette, France, and Liberty. For full ten minutes the enthusiasm continued unabated, the people's voice every now and then rising above the clamor of music and cannon. It was certainly a most thrilling scene and one to remember.[30]

Bartholdi's Marriage in the United States and the Completion of the Fund-Raising Campaign in France

Auguste Bartholdi was not to rest on his laurels after the unveiling of Lafayette, but he preserved the laurel wreath he received on this occasion. The publicity he got because of the ceremony was only a help towards the greater goal he had set: the erection of Liberty on Bedloe's Island. He felt that failure in this project would expose him to ridicule. However, he never gave any indication that he regretted being involved in the gigantic task; on the contrary he did not let an opportunity go by to work on it. Now he was famous. Invitations were coming to him from all sides. On September 19 he was received at the Lotos Club of New York and had a chance to talk about his Statue. On the 24th of the same month he wrote to his mother from Philadelphia that the arm of Liberty was having much effect and that he would like to take advantage of this to have subscriptions for the Pedestal started. "The spark is missing," he said.[1] At the same time he added that he hoped that the forthcoming dinners would give results. Before that spark came to set things in motion, however, the sculptor was in for a rude shock. On September 29, 1876, *The New York Times* published an ironical editorial entitled *The French Statue*. Incited by some false rumors that work on the Statue of Liberty had been suspended in France after $200,000 had been collected and all the amount used for the arm and torch erected in Philadelphia, the New York newspaper stated that the news of the gift of the Statue had at first been received gladly, although with some incredulity. Finally, it continued, the arm had arrived with the "thumb-nail affording an easy seat for the largest fat woman now in existence."[2] The editorial also stated that Americans were now expected to pay for the rest of the Statue, and that if it had cost $200,000 to make an arm the other arm would cost a like amount, each leg probably $250,000, and so forth. The newspaper estimated that the whole Statue would cost at least $2,000,000. The editorial pointed out jokingly that it had been argued that to start a statue by making one arm was not the proper way, although it added:

a woman without arms might be of considerable value. In Western towns where husbands yearn after the privilege of safely wearing long hair such a woman would be especially eligible for matrimonial purposes.[3]

The writer of the editorial also wrote that if the sculptor had really wanted to complete the Statue, he would have started modeling a foot, then a leg — not an arm — and sent over gradually all the other parts of the body to be successively unveiled. The editorial concluded thus:

It would inquestionably be impolitic to look a gift statue in the mouth, but inasmuch as no mouth has yet been cast for the bronze Liberty, we may be permitted to suggest that when a nation promises to give another nation a colossal bronze woman, and then, after having given one arm, calmly advises the recipient of that useless gift to supply the rest of the woman at his own expense, there is a disproportion between the promise and its fulfilment which may be forgiven, but which cannot be wholly ignored.[4]

There was no reference in the article that America was only to provide the money for the Pedestal with the French providing the necessary amount for the Statue itself.

This editorial from *The New York Times* was brought to the attention of Bartholdi who was particularly nettled by two statements, namely that he had taken out a contract to complete the Statue and that the work would cost the large amount referred to by the newspaper. *The Press* of Philadelphia published his reply to *The New York Times*. On October 5 this Philadelphia daily paper first published a lengthy account of a dinner given two days before in honor of Liberty's arm, then Bartholdi's reply which will be dealt with in due course.

The hosts at this dinner were the members of the committee of French exhibitors at the Centennial Exhibition and the guest of honor was Auguste Bartholdi. The dinner was served at *Les Trois Frères Provençaux,* a French restaurant located on the exhibition grounds near the artificial lake, and one could see from it Liberty's arm and torch brightly illuminated. Bartholdi's work was praised in speeches and toasts. Forney, who represented the American press, stated that the Statue of Liberty was the only object presented by a foreign power to the United States on the occasion of the Centennial. He expressed regret that the Statue would not be in Philadelphia and the thought that if ever New York — a case which he felt sure would not occur — could not raise the money, the Philadelphians would do so and place it in Fairmount Park. Mayor William H. Wickham of New York City had been invited to attend the dinner, but he could not make it and had sent Mr. Page to represent him and read a letter from him. The contents of this letter showed that not everyone in New York shared the views of *The New York Times.* The Mayor wrote in flattering terms about Bartholdi and his Statue and about New York's appreciation of France's gesture. The letter said:

When New York harbor shall be illuminated and adorned by the colossal figure of which a piece of the arm is before you today, we shall feel that this city is indeed exalted among all the cities of the world by modern art.[5]

After reading the letter Mr. Page recalled the enthusiasm which had greeted the recent unveiling of Bartholdi's statue of Lafayette in New York, an occasion also alluded to in the mayor's letter.

After the report concerning the dinner *The Press* published in full "with deep humiliation that a cause should exist for it, Monsieur Bartholdi's noble letter to *The New York Times.*"[6] *The Press* referred to the New York paper's "unjust and ungallant strictures on the great sculptor's work."[7]

In his letter Bartholdi emphasized that he was acting on behalf, not of himself, but of the French committee headed by Laboulaye. This committee had undertaken to raise money for Liberty which would cost 600,000 francs or about $120,000. The artist wrote that until he read the article of September 29 in the New York paper he had been convinced that the names of Lafayette, Rochambeau, Laboulaye, Tocqueville, and Noailles, who were connected with the project, were respected in the United States and that he felt sorry that the newspaper did not understand. He continued:

I now await the action of the American people whether the work itself shall or shall not be established on Bedloe's Island by the generous co-operation of your country.[8]

Bartholdi defended himself against the intimation that he expected to make money out of a contract and stated that this was his second stay in the United States "at my own expense." In conclusion Bartholdi said that he had received many generous words from most of the newspapers in New York that "I am loth to believe that they share your own feeling."

In his letter to *The New York Times* the artist also referred to a committee formed in Philadelphia to raise money in order to keep Liberty's arm in that city as a permanent exhibit. He naturally added that Philadelphia, so hospitable to him, would welcome the whole monument which would stand as a symbol of the "fulfilled promises and prophecies of the Declaration of Independence." The letter was written in a very restrained style which did credit to the writer and to the person who helped him put it into good English. *The Press* gave the names of all the people on the committee formed to purchase the arm and torch, with no money going to the artist, but only to the French firms which had made it. Nothing came of this because the arm was taken to New York and exhibited there, and later returned to France in order to be incorporated in the Statue of Liberty.

The sculptor went to New York shortly after the dinner referred to in *The Press* and, although election campaigns absorbed his friends' interest for a while, he was able to write to his mother:

Things are coming along fine. I can say the execution of the large Statue is now assured, and when all that is necessary is done I shall leave with my mind at rest, confident in the future.[9]

At a reception given by the Palette Association, a large picture by Edward Moran was exhibited showing "Liberty Lighting the World's Commerce." This picture, which is also sometimes called "The Commerce of Nations Paying Hommage to Liberty," represented the Statue surrounded by ships, flying the flags of many nations. It had been authorized by Bartholdi, a newspaper stated.[10] The artist was very pleased with the reception and with the painting which, he wrote to his mother, would be shown at the Paris Exhibition. "All will go well" he added, "and I shall have at least the satisfaction of coming back victorious."[11] He also remarked that he was expecting to return to Europe at the end of November 1876.

Although some newspapers in the United States continued to oppose the erection of the Statue of Liberty, the comments of the press were more and more favorable. The *Boston Globe* said that 125 French cities and towns had already subscribed to the Statue of Liberty Fund and that committees were being formed all over the country to support the project.[12] *The Daily Graphic* sang Bartholdi's praise in these words:

There is no instance except this of a nation rearing a statue in the ground and for the honor of another. . . M. Bartholdi volunteered his services as a sculptor and entered upon his work without hope of reward beyond that which would accrue to him from the artistic excellence of the work he should accomplish.[13]

Now that everything was appearing to be well under way in the United States, Madame Bartholdi back in Alsace was beginning to wonder whether there was not some other reason besides the Statue of Liberty business for keeping her Auguste away from her for such a long time. *"Cherchez la femme,"* they sometimes say, and all of a sudden you find her. In a letter from Newport the sculptor approached the subject very carefully:

You have asked: "Is there not a cousin at the LaFarges?" Yes, there is one, but would you like her? I think that you would in some respects, but this is no brilliant match. There is neither wealth, nor beauty, nor society connections, nor musical talents. Yet, she has the most likable features — a heart of gold which reflects itself on her face.[14]

Auguste went on revealing for the first time to his mother in this letter that he had been quite ill during the summer on account of the climate and of his worries about the Statue of Liberty project. He had gone to Canada in order to find a less enervating climate. While he was in Montreal, where he had become so ill that he had to call a doctor and send a telegram to John LaFarge in Newport, something did happen. . . One day the hotel bellboy came to his room to tell him that a lady sent by Mr. LaFarge wanted to see him, "and I see a kind and smiling face entering my room like a ray of sunshine."[15] The lady who lived in Montreal was a relative of Mrs. LaFarge. Bartholdi had met her in Newport on the occasion of his first trip to the United States in 1871, but had not paid special attention to her. He had not seen her since that time. When she cordially shook his hand: "It gave me a deep feeling of comfort. I felt as if she had been sent by you. She stayed with me until the next day."[16] Later that cousin went to Newport, and stayed there for a whole month, during which Bartholdi and she saw one another each day.

After thus preparing his mother for more revelations, the artist finally gave the cousin's name and background. Jeanne-Emilie was thirty-six years old and had had a rather sad life. Born in France, a daughter of a well-to-do manufacturer who later lost his fortune, she had become an orphan at the age of six. She had two sisters older than she. These sisters had married and died, one in Australia and the other in Marseilles. She had been adopted by a relative or friend of Canadian origin by the name of Mrs. Walker and had lived in Paris with her adoptive mother until 1871. Jeanne-Emilie had left Paris for Montreal with Mrs. Walker at the time when the French capital was recovering from the Franco-Prussian War and the Commune. This was about the time when Bartholdi had taken his first trip to the United States and explains why they had met in Newport in 1871. The artist had met Mrs. Walker at the same time. This lady, the artist wrote in his letter, had died without leaving a will making provisions for Jeanne-Emilie. Fortunately some of Mrs. Walker's heirs had provided Jeanne-Emilie with a small pension. Mrs. Walker, Bartholdi added, had been rather "selfish" (in English in the letter). She had taken the little girl as one takes a nice pet dog and had cared very little about giving her an education. She had refused to let her marry wanting to keep her all for herself. The young woman had learned on her own, studying the piano. On account of the fact that she had missed a carefree youth, the slightest pleasure made her happy. When she smiled she looked only twenty years old. In this unusually long letter the sculptor explained to his mother that all he was after was tender and devoted affection and that ambition should apply to work only, not to marriage. Jeanne-Emilie's only ambition was to feel that she was loved. Bartholdi added that the LaFarges who had him meet several young ladies, including a Boston heiress, were afraid that Madame Bartholdi would think that such a match was too modest for her beloved Auguste who was an artist of renown.

Bartholdi went on to say in his letter: "If you harbor any doubt or regret, I could not be happy. Tell me frankly. I am perfectly able to control myself."[17] The sculptor then wrote that the reason why he had not written to his mother about this before was in order not to have to tell her that he had been ill. He enclosed a photograph of Jeanne-Emilie, taken when she was not aware of it. Since the picture did not show the whole person, the artist, who was not particularly tall himself, specified that she was *petite*. Bartholdi concluded his letter by asking his mother to send him a telegram as soon as she had recovered from the shock this news was bound to give her. He promised that he would follow her advice.

This letter and the following ones about the same matter, as well as a number of cables of which Madame Bartholdi kept copies in a box, throw an entirely new light on the sculptor's relationship with the woman who was to become his wife.[18] This letter was followed by another dated Montreal, November 3, and starting in this manner: "I can imagine the shock my last letter must have caused you."[19] Bartholdi explained that he had gone to Canada to visit Miss de Puysieux and thank her for all she had done for him when he was there during the summer. This letter thus gives Jeanne-Emilie's last name, or at least the aristocratic-sounding part of it. Her full name was Jeanne-Emilie Baheux de Puysieux. She liked to be called just Jeanne and was usually designated in Bartholdi's letter by this name. He wrote that the family with whom she had been living for the last two months was about to leave for Chicago. The children had given her much pleasure, and Bartholdi wrote that he was worried about her spending the winter all alone. The sculptor, who had not had time to receive anything from Colmar about his mother's reaction, added that he feared that she might think Jeanne was not young enough for him. At the time the artist was a little over forty-two, while Jeanne was thirty-six. He also suggested that Madame Bartholdi might get some information about her from the LaFarges. In conclusion he promised that he would not mention her again in his letters until he had heard from his mother.

The shock must have been very great indeed for Madame Bartholdi in Colmar. Her Auguste whom she had always followed so closely was getting involved in a love affair with a woman she had never met, far away in America. She must have read the two letters several times. There was something that she would have liked to know and that her son had omitted in his account of Jeanne's background. She could not find it in any of the letters. So when she had recovered from her surprise, she went to the telegraph office and sent a cable with these words: "If one is a Catholic defer the outcome."[20] Just this and her name. Bartholdi had voluntarily or unvoluntarily neglected the all important matter of Jeanne's religion. From what her son had written about her education Madame Bartholdi could have inferred that the religious side had also probably been neglected. However, was she not living in Montreal, French Canada, that "hotbed" of Roman Catholicism! If her Auguste was to marry he should get a young lady from a good Protestant family. The involvement of Auguste's brother with a Jewish woman had led to complications which have already been referred to. She felt that it was essential for her son's happiness that he should marry a woman of the same faith as his. Probably after consulting with a local minister Bartholdi solved the problem of Jeanne's religion. "She is a Protestant," he wrote to his mother, "a Unitarian. This simply means a reasonable Protestant. Unitarians are for the unity of God."[21] The chances are that Jeanne at that time did not belong to any denomination at all, but at least she had not been brought up in the Roman Catholic faith, and this was certainly a relief to Madame Bartholdi. In that letter the sculptor reaffirmed that he did not want to marry a selfish or apathetic woman, but one who would give him affection and comfort in the ups and downs of an artist's life. Many

54

words were underlined in this letter and Bartholdi stressed that he did not care what the world might think of this match.

No trace could be found of the letter which Madame Bartholdi sent after being informed about Jeanne's religious affiliation; but from a letter her son wrote it appears that she would have liked to meet Jeanne before giving her approval, that she would have liked her to come to Europe, and most likely to have a wedding in Colmar. When her son explained that this was not possible, she must have sent a letter which puzzled her Auguste and she endeavored to set things right by sending a cable on November 19: "Happy, satisfied, agree, approve of marriage, a second letter will explain."[22] Under such circumstances Bartholdi felt that he could risk another visit to Newport where Jeanne was staying as a guest of the LaFarge family. When she saw him she burst into tears. Then Mrs. LaFarge also started crying, and the sculptor himself could not hold back his tears because of the emotion he felt at this reunion.[23] Yet, Jeanne was worried about the age difference between her and Bartholdi and thought that Madame Bartholdi must have dreamed of another marriage for her artist son. She was afraid that her future mother-in-law might not like her. So she finally decided to write to her. This letter has been preserved. It is a touching letter, and the author cannot resist giving most of its contents, although it is not easy to render the full meaning in translation.

Newport, December 10, 1876.

Very honored and dear Madam:

I am still under the charm of what Mr. Bartholdi has told me. So you agree with his project; you approve of it completely!

I cannot believe in such a happiness! I, the companion of his life! It is a dream! I am so happy that I am afraid. I have not anything of brilliance to offer the world. I am very anxious to perfect myself in order to be worthy of him. I have never received the care which all children get. I had to be serious at an early age and to hide within my heart youthful impulses. I have never experienced any tender affection except from my very dear friend and cousin Mrs. LaFarge. . .

I have only my heart. It beat very hard when I saw him again. . . Mrs. LaFarge tells me that you will like me. If I am to embrace you like a daughter, I beg you to be kind and lenient towards me who would like to love you with all my heart. You will help me, won't you? I have seen your picture which tells me that you must be kind like your son. Let me kiss you with all my heart.

Jeanne Baheux de Puysieux.[24]

This was the first of a great many letters from Jeanne to Madame Bartholdi which were kept like those of Auguste in envelopes. The subsequent correspondence between the son and the mother show that the latter still had mental reservations about the forthcoming wedding. She made another effort to have the wedding in Alsace. "Impracticable. Read again letter No. 28, answer, shall come back end of January," said a cable from New York dated December 12, 1876. Bartholdi appears to have been once again very occupied with the Statue of Liberty business. However, he could foresee when he would be able to leave. He did leave in January 1877.

The date of the wedding was set, and Bartholdi sent the following cable to his mother: "Tomorrow, Wednesday, four o'clock afternoon in Colmar, bless Jeanne Auguste."[25] The wedding ceremony was performed on December 20 in the LaFarge home at Newport by Reverend Charles T. Brooks, described as "a writer of merit and the minister of the Unitarian Church in Newport." Jeanne was presented as "the niece of a distinguished American artist, Mr. John LaFarge."[26] Only the family attended the wedding. The newlyweds expected a cable from Madame Bartholdi giving them her blessing. The artist and his mother often exchanged cables. But nothing came on December 20, December 21 went by; still no cable. On December 22 Bartholdi decided to write not to send a cable. His mother in Colmar had the same thought on the same day, and she mailed a letter dated December 22 to her Auguste. She must have pondered very carefully what she was going to write because she kept the rough copy of her letter. She explained that when she was in the telegraph office about to send her cable she had a fit and was unable to do anything. She would have like so much, she wrote "to be with her Auguste at this most solemn moment of his life."[27] She then mentioned that she had not received any information about the wedding, the church, the city hall, the guests, and so forth. She added that she now loved Jeanne because "she is my Auguste's companion." Madame Bartholdi must have been very upset indeed. This is shown by the number of slips of paper she scribbled in her attempt to write a cable for her son's wedding. She did not know what to say. Which one of these slips did she finally take to the telegraph office when she had her fit? Did she ever remember? Now it had happened and she decided to make the best of it and had wedding announcements printed in French to be sent to friends and relatives. A number of these have been preserved. Jeanne is presented as Mademoiselle Jeanne-Emilie de Puysieux, thus leaving out the non-aristocratic part of her name, and the name LaFarge is spelled La Forge. Certainly this was not the way she had visualized her Auguste's marriage, but what could be done now? It was all over without her having been there. At that time many things must have come to her mind, including her announcement to her friends several years before of her son's engagement to a young lady she personally knew. Nothing had come of this. The artist had not been ready for marriage at that time, but that would have been a match she would have been proud of. The existence of information concerning this previous marriage project — which was mentioned earlier — shows that one could not accuse Madame Bartholdi of not wanting her son to marry in order to keep him for herself. She once had him nearly married off, and while he was in Bordeaux she had hoped that he would make connections with some of the good Protestant families of the city. There is no doubt that when she later found out that the wedding had not taken place in a church and had not been surrounded by all the trimmings of bourgeois society she was not particularly pleased. The marriage announcements which she had had printed at least saved appearances to a certain extent.[28]

Although personal matters had taken much of Bartholdi's time and had filled quite a bit of his correspondence from October on, he had never stayed in Montreal or Newport very long, always coming back to New York or Philadelphia to foster the Statue of Liberty campaign. He once wrote: "One cannot imagine all I have had to do and especially to wait, it was like the cooking of a poor crawfish."[29] The artist was continuing to go from one meeting to the other. On January 2, 1877 he attended one of these at the Century Club in New York City. The list of names given by the newspapers of the people who were at that meeting indicated that "The American Committee on the Statue of Liberty" was already in the process

of formation with William Evarts, a prominent lawyer and statesman, as chairman, John Jay, Richard Butler, F. R. Coudert, Judge
Hilton, Joseph Choate, Henry Spaulding, Samuel Babcock, Theodore Roosevelt, and a number of others as members.[30] The great
canvas by E. Moran, entitled "Liberty Lighting the World's Commerce," had been borrowed for the occasion and was hanging behind the chairman's seat. A poem by John Moran was read, one of
the first of the numerous poems inspired by the Statue of Liberty.
William Evarts narrated the story of the project in France and said
that the American share was to be about $125,000. It was found
subsequently that the Pedestal and its foundation, which were the
American share of the project, would cost about double that amount.
One of the reasons for this discrepancy, as was discovered later, was
that the engineers had not been given enough time to prepare their
estimates.

Evarts suggested the formation of a committee of twenty members.
Colonel Hawkins asked for a petition to be sent to the New York
legislature requesting an allocation to bolster private donations. This
proposal was opposed by Parke Godwin, F. R. Coudert, and Judge
Noah Davis. They claimed that the undertaking would lose its
popularity if taxpayers over the whole of New York State were to
be involved. It appeared that this opinion prevailed for the time
being, and it was decided to leave the matter in the hands of the
future committee. Mr. Evarts was asked to form that committee after
he had approached individually possible members in order to find
out their intentions. Bartholdi was, of course, among the speakers
of the evening. After all the waiting he must have been quite re-
lieved to see the way things were shaping, and on January 8 he
was pleased to be able to write to his mother: "The matter of the
Statue of Liberty is finally solved; the committee is organized."[31]

This was really a great achievement; yet there was still one more
thing which detained him in the United States — the monumental
fountain built for the Centennial Exhibition. He wrote from
Albany, in up-state New York, that he was trying to sell it there, but
that it looked as if it was going to take a while and that he would
probably have to take steps to have it sold after his departure on
January 27.[32] The fountain was finally sold in Washington D.C., and

it is the one which still plays on Capitol Hill near the new Rayburn House Office Building.

Naturally Bartholdi's last letters from the United States also mentioned Jeanne, who was about to have to face her mother-in-law for the first time. The artist wrote:

Her only concern is to have your affection. This is her *point noir* (black spot). As soon as she is sure that you love her she will be the happiest human being on earth. On Christmas Day when we left church she told me: "I did not understand the minister, but I prayed all the time for your mother to like me."[33]

While in Albany he wrote that he was looking forward to returning home to find his good Jeanne waiting for him. "It seems to me that I find the other half of you."

The steamship *La France* of the *Compagnie Générale Transatlantique* docked in Plymouth on February 6, 1877 with the Bartholdis aboard. The next day the artist sent a telegram from Le Havre announcing that the couple would be in Colmar on Sunday, after a rest in Paris. After the announcement of the marriage Madame Bartholdi had taken a trip to Paris to make the sculptor's bachelor home ready for the bride. A maid had been looking after the place during Bartholdi's absence, but the touch of someone who knew was needed.

This second trip to the United States had been very different from the first one. The artist had seen much less of the country than in 1871. He had stayed in the East all the time. The Statue of Liberty had not been ready for the Centennial, yet the trip could be called a success. After a long period of waiting the Statue's arm and torch had finally appeared at the Exhibition. Several works by Bartholdi had been exhibited there, including the large fountain in a very good location. The two certificates of awards the artist got for sculpture are still to be seen in Colmar.[34]

Bartholdi also prepared a report on the fine arts which was published after his return in France. Some of the remarks he made in this seventeen-page publication are interesting. The artist not only spoke about what he saw in Philadelphia, but he also drew on his impressions of the country as a whole which he had gained during his 1871 trip to the West Coast. He said, for instance, that there were four stages in the growth of American cities. The first consisted of frame structures, while the last, symbolizing acquired prosperity, displayed marble and granite.[35] He felt that customs and institutions had not made it possible to give to American cities and monuments the great decorative aspects that architecture gave European cities, but that Americans had great freedom of action. In his report the artist expressed surprise at some American ways; for instance that coffins were displayed at the Centennial and that they were to be seen in the windows of some stores. While the report contained some criticisms of the United States, it fully recognized the merits of all that had been achieved in a relatively short period of time — one hundred years.

With his Statue of Liberty probably in mind Bartholdi also pointed out in his report that Americans can be very generous for the arts. On his second trip Bartholdi had come into contact with some of the right people to support the Statue of Liberty campaign. Although, as will be seen, money for the Pedestal was not to come in easily, a committee had been formed which could correspond with its French counterpart, the *Union Franco-Américaine* in Paris. Last but not least Bartholdi had met the woman who was to share his joys and sorrows as an artist and as a man. Now there was another woman in his life besides his beloved mother.

Shortly after the sculptor and his wife arrived in France the final organization of the American Committee on the Statue of Liberty was announced. There were to be five subcommittees. The first one, under Evarts's chairmanship, was to issue a national appeal; the second, under Babcock's leadership, was to cooperate with the chambers of commerce; the third, with Avery, was to have charge of publicity; the fourth, again with Evarts, was to insure contacts with Congress; while the fifth, with Weston as its chairman, was to look after the erection of the Statue of Liberty. There was also a committee in Boston.[36] This organization was to be modified as time went on, some subcommittees ceasing to function, while others came into being, such as an executive committee and a finance committee. The Boston committee was not very active, the main support coming from the New York area.

Another great step towards Bartholdi's goal was taken when on February 22, 1877 Congress accepted unanimously the gift of the

Statue of Liberty from France. The artist hailed the news and wrote from Paris to his mother: "I also have news of the large Statue business. The impulse I have given continues to gain momentum. Let's hope that this time Fortune will be smiling for some time."[37] After the close of the Centennial Exhibition Liberty's arm with the torch was sent to New York and was erected at the intersection of Fifth Avenue and Broadway. There was a charge of 50 cents to ascend the steel ladder leading to the balcony around the torch. The arm stayed there until it was shipped back to France.

Bartholdi was now having frequent American visitors in his Paris studio. Among these was Richard Butler, who later served as secretary of the American Committee on the Statue of Liberty, and was to have an extensive correspondence with Bartholdi. Butler's son-in-law, Georges Glaenzer, was a Frenchman whose family, judging by the name, might have originally come from Alsace, Bartholdi's home province. Glaenzer resided in Paris, but often came to New York. He was in the fine wines and luxury articles business and often served as an intermediary between Bartholdi and his friends in New York. Some of these American visitors were nuisances, and the artist wrote that once he had trouble getting rid of one of them.[38]

When the sculptor was too busy to write long letters, his wife Jeanne wrote about what was going on. She was so proud to see her Auguste "surrounded by active friendships and feelings that he deserves so much."[39] This author has not come across any information about the first meeting of the artist's mother with her daughter-in-law, but judging from the subsequent correspondence between the two women they appear to have got along all right and evidently Madame Bartholdi senior was not annoyed that she no longer was the only woman in her son's life. On the contrary she seemed to have done all she could to make the couple comfortable, often sending them delicacies from Alsace, such as goose liver and fruit.

Although Bartholdi occasionally took time off to go to a Normandy beach, he was so creative at this period that he was usually busy working on models and monuments. Some of these were unveiled before the Statue of Liberty was ready. His Lion of Belfort, already mentioned, was unveiled in 1880. The completion of the Statue of Liberty was no longer a matter of creation, but of skill and precision, as each part of the model was being enlarged to its final size. Moreover, all the necessary funds had not been raised yet.

Great encouragement from the American side came on the last day of October 1877. General Grant, whom Bartholdi had met on his first trip to the United States when Grant was President, came to visit the workshop of the Statue of Liberty. Laboulaye and many members of the *Union Franco-Américaine* were on hand for this great occasion which was sure to get publicity in France as well as in the United States. The artist wrote: "I showed and explained our work to the General, and he looked with much interest, speaking little as is his habit."[40] Refreshments were served and the General was given a little terra-cotta reproduction of the Statue of Liberty to take with him as a souvenir of his visit. As soon as she read about the presence of such an important American visitor in Paris, Madame Bartholdi wrote to her son and her daughter-in-law, suggesting they should invite Grant to their home. Usually very responsive to his mother's suggestions the artist did not follow them this time. He replied that he and Jeanne did not think that it would look right to do this. He added that he knew how to make his influence felt without putting himself forward and causing envy. This was what he did:

Yesterday I attended the great banquet offered to the General. My influence was felt without anyone noticing it. I arranged for some necessary people to be invited. I had a painting exhibited representing the monument and so forth. . ., but as for myself I was standing aside so that my efforts would benefit the work.[41]

During former President Grant's visit Bartholdi was able to sell one of his statues which he had "strategically" placed in the hall leading to a ballroom. He was going to put another one there.[42] Whether this one was sold too we do not know. Statuary does not sell as easily as ordinary merchandise. There is no doubt, however, that Bartholdi was not only a productive artist, but also a good business man. He was the one who did get things going for the Statue of Liberty, both in France and in America, especially in America, because his stake in it was greater than that of the people who helped him. He was not just commissioned to execute a statue someone else had suggested. The chances are that without him the idea of a monument to Franco-American friendship would have remained a suggestion. Not only this, but for a time he was the only secretary of the *Union Franco-Américaine* doing all the letter writing for the organization.[43] General Grant was later to write a letter of appreciation to Laboulaye, president of the *Union,* concerning his visit to the workshop. It was dated November 21, and Laboulaye's reply was sent the following day. Both have been preserved.

During the year 1878 the highlight of the work on Liberty was the setting up of the Statue's head at the Paris Universal Exhibition. A reporter who wrote about it said that what was striking in the enlarged head was an expression of rigidity, of seriousness, and even harshness which was not noticeable in the smaller model. He added that this first impression disappears when one gets nearer to the Statue. He continued: "A few mallet knocks will remove this: the sculptor does not hide the fact that he wants to give an impression of firmness to the face."[44] As in the case of the arm with the torch arrangements were made for people to climb into the head, as they are able to do today after going through the whole Pedestal and body of the Statue. In Paris the trip was much shorter, just a few steps to go up and one was there. Admission was charged as a help toward the fund for the Statue.

Quite a bit of money had still to be raised in France in order to go ahead with the work on Liberty. So, following a license obtained from the Ministry of the Interior on May 9, 1879, a large lottery was organized to be held on June 27 on the premises of the *Magasins Réunis,* a large department store located on the *Château d'Eau* Square in Paris. The license authorized the issue of 300,000 lottery tickets at one franc each. In those days the French franc was already worth less than the dollar. There were many valuable prizes — the first was a silver plate set, worth 20,000 francs; the second a piece of jewelry made of pearls and brilliants, worth 5,000 francs. The 528 prizes included some works of art. Bartholdi contributed a terracotta of his Vauban. This was one of the models he had made of the great French military engineer for the city of Avallon, Vauban's birthplace, a few years earlier. The artist also donated a painting called *La Vague* (The Wave). The lottery got a grand opening with the traditional speeches. Senator Bozérian, one of the vice presidents of the *Union Franco-Américaine,* recalled that the appeal was launched in 1875, and expressed regret that the Statue of Liberty was not ready for 1876, for the July 4 celebration. The historian Henri Martin also spoke, giving full credit to Bartholdi for getting the project going. He justified the use of a lottery to raise money for such a worthwhile cause.

Another method used by the *Union Franco-Américaine* to raise money for the Statue of Liberty was the selling of small clay models, called "Models of the Committee," touched up and signed by the artist. Each of these statuettes had the Committee's seal and a number. Moreover, each purchaser of one of these models which sold for one thousand francs in France and three hundred dollars in the United States, had his or her name, as well as the model's number, entered in a so-called "Golden Book of the Subscription." In addition purchasers could have their names engraved in the clay before the model was put into the oven to be baked. A number of these models still exist in the United States, and elsewhere.

By the end of 1879 the equivalent of about $250,000 in French money had been raised, and on July 7, 1880 the members of the *Union Franco-Américaine* gathered for breakfast at the Hotel Continental in Paris to sign an illuminated parchment, which officially announced that the Statue of Liberty would be completed in 1883. This parchment was sent to the United States and is preserved in the Manuscript Division of the New York Public Library, while a photograph of the original is in the *Musée Bartholdi* in Colmar. There are about forty signatures on it including the names of a descendant of Lafayette, of Bartholdi, Laboulaye, Lesseps, Bozérian, and Stucklé. The parchment tells in French about the meeting at which the notification was made, the place where Liberty will stand, and its meaning:

Thus will live on, consecrated by the imperishable bronze, the glorious memory of the friendship of the two nations, a friendship sealed by the blood of their fathers.[45]

Although the Statue of Liberty was in copper the parchment referred to bronze, a nobler metal. The document also said that the French manifestation of friendship was supported by 181 towns and cities, represented by the votes of their councils, by the chambers of commerce of ten of the most important cities in France, and 100,000 signatures of individual subscribers.

The signing of this document and its sending to the United States was an important step for the French share of the Statue of Liberty project, but it will be seen that disappointment and doubt were to arise when this action did not meet with the hoped-for reaction on the other side of the Atlantic.

CHAPTER FIVE

The Fund-Raising Campaign Begins in the United States and the Statue of Liberty is Completed in France

The *Union Franco-Américaine* gave itself three years to complete the Statue of Liberty. This was an indication that they fully realized what a mammoth job it represented, and no one knew this better than Bartholdi himself. In this connection an article by Charles Lefèbre which appeared in 1881 is of interest. Lefèbre went to see Bartholdi in his studio on Vavin Street and admired a miniature reproduction of the whole workshop where the head had been made. It was complete, including the modest broom used to sweep the shop, with the workers and Bartholdi himself giving instructions. "Monsieur Bartholdi," Lefèbre wrote, "like the artists of the Renaissance, believes that a sculptor is not complete unless he is also an architect."[1] About the Statue of Liberty the writer of the article explained that, although the idea was excellent, it was not at all easy to carry it out, and he added:

To erect this colossus the artist had no other strength but his faith in his work; no other support but his patriotism. He did not become disheartened. Full of this contagious ardor and confidence in success which only a strong faith can give, he finally got others to share his idea. He gathered around him all those who, for one reason or another, were anxious to strengthen the old alliance between America and France. . . The *Union Franco-Américaine* was organized with artistic aims, but its purpose was also to commemorate a great historical event. Bartholdi was the soul of

66

this enterprise, and one will never know all that it cost him in efforts, in negotiations, and thankless work.[2]

Starting with the year 1881 there is a new source of information about the work on the Statue of Liberty — the letters received by Richard Butler, secretary of the American Committee on the Statue of Liberty, from Auguste Bartholdi and others. The file has been deposited in the Manuscript Division of the New York Public Library. The first of these letters was signed by J. W. Pinchot, a member of the American Committee on the Statue of Liberty, who was visiting Paris. This letter referred to the meeting of July 7, 1880 when the parchment announcing that the Statue would be completed in 1883 was signed by many "distinguished Republicans of France."[3] Pinchot wrote that the parchment had been sent to Mr. Evarts through Paul Noyes, the American minister to France, but that the document had never been acknowledged, and that such a gesture would be an encouragement for the French Committee. One cannot help wondering what happened to the parchment between July 7, 1880, when it was signed, and January 10, 1881, the date of Pinchot's letter. Lost at the bottom of the diplomatic bag? One may assume that it must have reached the American Committee. Anyway, it is quite safe in New York. A second letter from Pinchot said that the Statue of Liberty was expected to be ready for the 1883 World Fair.[4] Writing to Butler again on April 5 Pinchot said that Bartholdi was very anxious for the American Committee on the Statue of Liberty to meet before Evarts' projected departure for France, "in order to show the friends of the Statue that some interest is being taken in what is being done."[5] The letter added that the plaster model, one quarter the size of the final Statue, was now in the workshop where Liberty would rise and that the number of workmen would be increased to thirty in a few weeks.

On October 24, 1881, on the hundredth anniversary of the surrender of Yorktown, which was brought about thanks to the assistance of French forces, a ceremony took place at the workshop of the Statue of Liberty on Chazelles Street. Levi P. Morton, American minister to France, was asked to drive the first rivet in the Statue of Liberty. The *Union Franco-Américaine* had felt that this was a suitable occasion to further cement the bonds of friendship between

67

the United States and France. The ceremony attracted much attention. On December 10 Morton wrote to Butler about the ceremony, asking what he could do in Paris to help the American Committee.[6] Later in the month Bartholdi wrote to Butler. This was the first of a series of letters from the sculptor. His letter had been translated from the French by Georges Glaenzer, Butler's son-in-law, Bartholdi claiming that he had forgotten the little English he knew. . . This letter was in reply to a request from the Pedestal architect, Richard M. Hunt, for information about the measurements of Liberty. To the letter were joined documents with calculations made by "our engineers" to be given to "men of experience."[7]

During the year 1882 Bartholdi's life was bothered by legal proceedings. He got involved in the fight concerning the condemnation of his house in order to build a street. His studio, which had an enlarged door for removing his large models,was also in this house. Bartholdi's mother had probably, as usual, spent some time with the couple during the spring, and there seems to have been some misunderstanding between the two women because in a letter to her the artist assured his mother that Jeanne was "very anxious to be loved, but that perhaps she does not have the talent to express her thoughts the way she would like to."[8] Bartholdi was also busy on his statue of Rouget de Lisle, composer of the *Marseillaise,* the French national anthem. He engraved the music of the hymn in the bronze and wrote jokingly about this:

This may be very interesting to the archeologists in one thousand years from now. They will scratch and decipher with a magnifying glass my scrawly handwriting. I am trying to make it as easy as possible for them by making the engraving as clear as I can.[9]

But the artist's main concern was the Statue of Liberty and he spent much time at the workshop. At the 1882 *Salon* he exhibited a drawing of the interior of the Statue. In July of that year the Statue's height having reached the level of the woman's knee cap, Bartholdi struck on the idea of giving a luncheon to a sizable group of people on a platform erected inside Liberty's right leg. The press commented on the event, and the publicity was very helpful. In one of the newspapers that described the luncheon there is also information about the making of the Statue, given in a language which the general public could understand. The newspaper explained the process in the following way:

Each part of the statue is prepared with the use of little wooden lathes which form an enormous cage of lattice work. On this framework is put a heavy layer of plaster on which the adjustments are made. Later, new wooden moulds called *gabarits* are set on this plaster, and it is on these moulds that the men working with copper operate bending the rigid metal along all the curves, even the most delicate ones. After the copper plates are thus prepared, they are strengthened by means of strong iron frames.[10]

The same newspaper suggested that Bartholdi should give explanatory lectures on Sundays charging admission. The men working on the Statue in the Gaget-Gauthier workshop on Chazelles Street were introduced by the newspaper. There was Simon, a sculptor "who directed work with real passion." There were Bergeret, the foreman of the copper beaters; Baron, the head of the moulders; and Eiffel, the engineer. This was the same Gustave Eiffel who was to erect the famous tower for the 1889 World Exhibition. Thanks to his skill the Statue of Liberty was made strong enough to withstand the most violent gales which might sweep New York harbor. Eiffel was about fifty years old at that time and relatively little information is available among Bartholdi's papers about his relationship with the sculptor, who did not seem to treat him any differently from his other collaborators.

All of these co-workers were naturally invited to attend the special luncheon in the leg of the Statue. Bartholdi had also invited representatives of the press and friends from his native Alsace. The artist spoke about the international significance of the work. Senator Hébrard, publisher of *Le Temps,* replied for the press, and Mr. Siebecker for the Alsatians "in stirring words which found an echo in all hearts." The newspaper continued: "We hasten to add that this get-together had nothing to do with politics, protests, or demands."[11] This referred to the meetings of people from Alsace-Lorraine who had left their homes in order not to live under German rule. This type of meetings in Paris and elsewhere was meant to keep alive the memory of the lost provinces. To these people, as to Bartholdi, the Statue of Liberty was to be more than a symbol of Franco-American friendship — it embodied their hopes that some day Alsace-Lorraine would regain the freedom to decide her fate. By this they naturally meant her return to France. To them Bartholdi was to become a hero, and when he visited the United States the artist was honored by organizations of people from Alsace-Lorraine, particularly from Alsace, who had settled in the United States. *L'Union Alsacienne* of New York is the oldest of these organizations.[12]

Shortly after that memorable luncheon in the leg of the Statue of Liberty, the artist and his wife left for a trip — part vacation, part business. First there was a visit in Colmar, in the old family home with Bartholdi's mother; then a cure at Schinznach in Switzerland, and a trip to Lons-le-Saulnier, on the French side of the Jura, to attend the unveiling of the Rouget de Lisle monument in the town where the composer was born. Bartholdi must have had a feeling of relief when this unveiling was finally over, because there had been some difficulties in connection with the monument, and the artist had to interrupt his stay in Switzerland to return to Paris in order to settle some matters.[13] On the occasion of that unveiling ceremony on August 28, 1882 the French government conferred upon Bartholdi the Cross of the Legion of Honor. He had stepped on the first rung of the ladder of this order when he was twenty-two, at the time of the unveiling of his Rapp in Colmar.

The treatment at Schinznach was a joke to Bartholdi who wrote:

I have already had another bath, and I am going to put out my tongue at the inhalation: There would be a pretty picture to draw at the inhalation gathering. One must put out one's tongue to breathe well, and then it is a matter of who puts it out the farthest. Sometimes the doctor comes to see if all his pupils put out their tongues the right way.[14]

Bartholdi wrote this letter to his mother on the stationary of Gaget-Gauthier, the firm which was building the Statue of Liberty. He did this in order to quieten his mother's worries about the progress of the project in which she knew her son was involved heart and soul. In October 1882 work on the Statue was behind schedule in the Chazelles Street workshop.[15]

The situation on the other side of the Atlantic did not look promising at all at this time. Richard Butler, secretary of the American Committee on the Statue of Liberty, was informed that the

French Committee members were nettled at all the sarcastic comments about the Statue of Liberty which often appeared in the American newspapers. They would have liked to get some indication as to how the American public was feeling about the project in order to communicate it to the French press and through the press to the people of France. This was all the more important since a critical moment had been reached, namely the *Union Franco-Américaine* was about to approach the French government with a request to obtain official transportation to the United States for Liberty. Many people were coming to visit the workshop. Special invitations were mailed by the *Union* Committee to prominent people, encouraging them to come and see the progress being made on the Statue. On these invitations they were told that their names had been entered in a special register together with those of the members of the Committee and co-workers. These guests and the people accompanying them had only to give their names to be admitted to the workshop.

The request for transportation of the Statue of Liberty to the United States referred to above seems to have aroused the American friends of the Statue, because letters later on stated that news from the American side was more encouraging. "They begin to be actively interested in our work,"[16] Bartholdi wrote to his mother about the Americans on November 22. About a month later Madame Bartholdi must have been rather pleased to read in a letter from her son that: "There has been a very enthusiastic meeting in New York and matters seem to be taking the right course."[17] Although the year 1882 was closing on a favorable note it was not easy to work under such conditions. Fortunately Bartholdi continued to be honored with orders for the statues of France's great men. In his Christmas letter to his mother he told her that he had received a commission to make a monument of Denis Diderot, the eighteenth century French writer, for the city of Langres, his birthplace. Bartholdi once wrote that his only ambition was "to engrave my name at the feet of great men and in the service of grand ideas."[18] In this respect he was largely successful, and the men he modeled lived in many periods of history. This involved research on the artist's part. When he was working on his Vercingétorix, the Gallic hero who tried unsuccessfully to stem the Roman advance, the sculptor visited some slaughterhouses in order to study and make drawings of the muscles of horses for the mount of the Gaul. In his library in Colmar there is a book about the anatomy of the horse, as well as many others on costumes for different periods. Now, there was a Diderot to make. At least, if the Statue of Liberty work was slow there were many other things to keep him busy, and he did not always stay in his studio or at the Liberty workshop. He wrote to his mother that he and his wife were planning to attend a Christmas service in a church and later on a special festive meeting of people from Alsace.[19]

The *Union Franco-Américaine's* plan, after it proved impossible to finish more than the arm and torch of Liberty for 1876, was to have the whole Statue completed and ready to be offered to the American people and government by 1883. However, the Statue was not presented until the following year and was unveiled two years later, in 1886. That delay was certainly not Bartholdi's fault. He worked on the project unceasingly, and it can now be said that he was the kingpin of the whole undertaking from the beginning to the end. Naturally he could not do everything alone and he had to reckon with many factors. Some of these concerned funds; others technical difficulties in the workshop, such as calculations which had to be very precise so that the enlarged sections of the Statue would fit together. Bartholdi wrote that:

There were in each course about three hundred large points and more than one thousand and two hundred secondary points, which represented for each course the work of establishing about nine thousand measurements.[20]

Bartholdi also had to reckon with the attitude of the people he had to work with in France and in the United States. Last but not least, he had to be concerned with the reactions of the public, especially the American public. The latter was expected to contribute toward the construction of the Pedestal on which Liberty was to stand. How the funds for the Pedestal were finally obtained makes a very interesting chapter in the story of the Statue of Liberty.

Although the organization of the American Committee on the Statue of Liberty went back to the year 1877 — when Bartholdi visited the United States for the second time — contributions were lagging. True, enough money had been obtained to start the work on the foundations of the Pedestal, but the future looked dim indeed. It was a great shock when the news was received early in March 1883 that Congress had rejected a request for an appropriation of $100,000 for the building of the Pedestal. Henry F. Spaulding, the Committee's treasurer, who got the information from Washington, commented that it was really a shame considering that Congress had appropriated $400,000 for the New Orleans Show, but had not given a single dollar for a project which concerned the whole country.[21] What actually had happened was that the Senate had attached the appropriation request to a Deficiencies Bill to which the House objected. A conference committee had dropped the whole bill, without making any exception for the relatively small amount asked for the Pedestal. The American Committee on the Statue of Liberty held an emergency meeting and considered the possibility of suspending work on the Pedestal.

The news of the plight of the American Committee struck a responsive cord in the heart of Joseph Pulitzer. This man who was of Hungarian Jewish origin, was on his way to becoming a big name in American journalism. He had come to the United States during the Civil War and had served in the Union Army. After the end of the war he had become a reporter for a leading German newspaper in the Midwest. He became part-owner of this newspaper, and was elected to the Missouri Legislature on the Republican ticket in 1869. He later was to become a Democrat, and very much so. He studied law and was admitted to the bar in Washington, continuing his connections with the journalistic profession which was to bring him fame. In 1878 he bought the *Saint Louis Dispatch,* merged it with another newspaper, and in 1883 he purchased *The World,* a New York paper. It was shortly after this transaction that he made his first attempt to help the fund-raising campaign for the Statue of Liberty.

Joseph Pulitzer published a vigorous editorial in *The World* on March 14, 1883 with the following message to the public: "The Bartholdi Statue will soon be on its way to New York. The great goddess comes with her torch held aloft to enlighten the world."[22] The editorial went on blaming the millionaires who spent money unneccessarily. "Who will save us from this National Disgrace?" was its conclusion. Two months later another editorial came out in the same vein. "More appropriate would be the gift of a Statue of Parsimony than a Statue of Liberty, if this is the appreciation we show of a friendly nation's sentiment and generosity."[23] If the rich would not react, what about the poor? At the same time the newspaper announced the opening of a popular subscription to help raise money for the Pedestal. It offered to acknowledge all sums received.

As promised *The World* soon started publishing copies of letters from people sending in money, although the amounts were rather small. By May 18, however, the sum of $135.75 had been raised. On the same day an extract from the *Commercial Gazette* of Cincinnati was published, claiming that if a midwestern city like Saint Louis, Cincinnati, or Chicago had only to furnish a pedestal the Statue would not have to wait for long. On May 21 an editorial in *The World* suggested the opening of dollar subscriptions all over the country, stating that: "the whole country should feel interested in providing a pedestal for the Bartholdi Statue."[24] Money came in very slowly, and the newspaper was starting to get impatient, feeling that the answer to the appeal was humiliating, and commented bitterly: "The statue should be placed on Montmatre where people are appreciative of liberty."[25] On June 1 *The World* published a letter from the treasurer of the American Committee on the Statue of Liberty in which Spaulding stated that the Statue of Liberty was a gift from all the people of France and that therefore the money for its Pedestal should come from all over the United States. The following day the newspaper gave an account of the reaction of artists to an inquiry as to how money for the Pedestal could be raised. Their opinion was that the matter should have been pushed when the arm of Liberty was still in New York and that, moreover, rich men could better afford to help than artists. This was one of several instances of the lack of interest and even hostility on the part of many artists for the Statue of Liberty as a work of art, an attitude which has not changed to this day. There is no doubt that some aspects of Bartholdi's work ran against certain currents in the field of art. Statues are often expected to express feelings, while the Statue of Liberty purposely does not express any. Liberty's face is smooth and serene as that of most of the statues of Classical Greece and their Roman copies. Bartholdi was well able to express any feeling he chose in his sculptures. For Liberty he selected the look which seemed to him the best for a statue which was to be enlarged to gigantic proportions. A statue with rough contours, as some of the modern ones have, would not have been suitable for this purpose. As Laboulaye had pointed out in his speech at the Paris Opera, the sculptor had not wanted to represent a Liberty "walking on corpses and holding an incendiary torch," but a Liberty at home and "holding a shining beacon." A French art critic wrote that Bartholdi was particularly successful in creating "symbolical statues, those which *inform* thought, as the philosophers of old used to say."[26] Many recognized in the Statue of Liberty the classical tradition on which the artist had been nurtured, as is shown by this little poem:

In simple splendor, like our flag unfurled,
The white charm of the Hellenic past outdone,
So may it stand, where men have learned to shun
The hell of nation against nation hurled,
Its structure fair uplifted in the sun
To shed memorial radiance over the world.[27]

The chances are that if Liberty, damaged, smaller in size, in marble, without arms or without head, had been excavated somewhere in the Mediterranean area, it would have been hailed as a great work of art by those same artists who criticized Bartholdi's work. Critical artists have yet to produce another Statue of Liberty.

The World went on publishing opinions as to how money could be raised. Alderman Thomas Foley stated that the government of the City of New York should provide its share for the Pedestal. A German saloon-keeper thought that the Statue would be a great thing and that the State, not the City, should put up the money. Others felt that this was up to the Federal Government or to those of the states of the Union to do it. Charles B. Davis, a butcher in Washington Market, New York, told a reporter of *The World* the following:

No one that I have talked to about it knows what design it is going to be, or anything at all. Why don't they let up an excitement about it and let the people see that they are in earnest? Nine out of every ten know nothing at all about the matter. I am certain that very few men in this market do, and they can, when they feel like it, put down their names and the pieces for nice little sums. I should advise the committee to show a little more energy.[28]

As a matter of fact the American Committee on the Statue of Liberty was far from idle. In June 1883 $3,500 was raised at an amateur performance in Madison Square Theatre. Also the Committee advertised for building stone in New England newspapers.[29]

The World's campaign to help raise money for the Pedestal of the Statue of Liberty fizzled out in June 1883. But this was only Joseph Pulitzer's first effort. He had been quick to realize that this was a waste of time and that neither his newspaper, which had a small circulation at that time, nor the American public was ready for more. When he launched his second campaign he did not stop until the goal of $100,000 was reached. It is this second campaign of *The World,* that of 1885, which is the better known one. Although *The World* no longer appealed for money, it continued to keep the public informed about the progress on the Statue of Liberty and its Pedestal.

On July 7, 1883, as a sequel to the hundredth anniversary celebration of the surrender of Yorktown which, as mentioned previously, was marked in Paris by the fixing of the first rivet in the Statue, a booklet was issued by William Evarts and Parke Godwin to appeal to the people for funds. This appeal said:

It will be a fitting close to those imposing ceremonies to give permanence, we might say eternity, to the memories awakened on the occasion, by the erection of this stupendous image of Liberty Enlightening the World.[30]

A few days later the American Committee on the Statue of Liberty held a meeting at 171 Broadway, at which General Stone, chief engineer for the construction of the Pedestal, reported that two thirds of the excavation for the Pedestal on Bedloe's Island was completed and that difficulties were being experienced in removing old cisterns and cells.

A reporter from *The World* visited Bedloe's Island in September 1883 to see what was being done. He was told that weather permitting the foundations for the Pedestal would be finished by December 1. Some details of interest to newspaper readers were given — salt water was used to mix cement; the stone came from Weehawken, New Jersey, and the sand from Staten Island, a large island in New York bay. The reporter wrote that the excavation, 16 feet deep and 93 feet square, was to be filled with solid concrete and that tons of coal found in the old fort would be used for engines to mix concrete. Some 50 men were living on the island and appeared to be busy. Drake and McGaw were the contractors for the work.[31] This shows that in spite of the setback resulting from the rejection by Congress of the $100,000 appropriation request earlier in the year, work had proceeded on the island. *The World's* campaign may have had something to do with this. Although very little money was collected the campaign had a moral effect.

All possible means were used to obtain funds. About this time small models of the Statue of Liberty in metal, imitating bronze, were sold to raise money. The exclusive right to make them was granted by Bartholdi to the firm Avoiron and Company in Paris. These models were separate from the terra cotta statuettes, already mentioned, which were touched up by the sculptor. The American Committee on the Statue of Liberty advertised these models in newspapers month after month with pictures, stating that the design of both the Statue and the Pedestal were protected by United States patents, and that the small statues could only be obtained from the Committee. Statuettes six inches high and bronzed cost one dollar, while the twelve-inch ones were five dollars.[32]

The booklet still exists which lists the subscriptions obtained by the American Committee on the Statue of Liberty.[33] It contains an extract of a report presented to the Committee by Chief Engineer Stone, dated November 12, 1884. Stone estimated that it would cost another $148,000 to finish the Pedestal and mount the Statue so that it could be inaugurated in September 1885. The booklet gives the address of the Committee as 25 Liberty Street, Room 32, New York. From this booklet one also learns that the Committee's structure had changed, but that Evarts remained as chairman, Butler, secretary, and Spaulding, treasurer. There was also an executive committee under the chairmanship of Joseph W. Drexel. The booklet is interesting because it shows the amounts subscribed. A total of $37,434.03 was represented by sums between $1,000 and $2,000 — substantial amounts. The total subscribed by November 10, 1884 was $161,489.85. There are three entries for sums of $5,000 and up — the first being Drexel, Morgan & Company, $5,000; the second called "Proceeds of Art Loan Exhibition, New York City," $13,674.00; and the third, an anonymous gift of $6,000 from "a friend to France." The booklet has forty pages, and in each section there are blank pages for additional amounts. Sums smaller than 100 dollars are not listed. Among the last entries is 100 dollars subscribed by 800 children from the New York Juvenile Asylum on Washington Heights. If money had continued coming in at a regular rate the chances are that things would have worked out the way Chief Engineer Stone had planned and the Statue could have been unveiled in 1885. But, as will be seen, the last $100,000 was the hardest to get.

Meanwhile, on the other side of the Atlantic, the French were behind schedule too. They had expected the Statue to be ready in 1883, but it was not completed until the following year. The *Union Franco-Américaine* was grieved by the loss of their president — Laboulaye died in 1883. He was the one who had directed Bartholdi's thoughts toward the Statue of Liberty and had given the prestige of his name to the organization that helped implement the project. Laboulaye was succeeded by Ferdinand de Lesseps, the builder of the Suez Canal whom Bartholdi had visited in Egypt in 1869. Lesseps became interested in the Statue of Liberty very early, maybe to make up for the little encouragement he had given to the sculptor when the latter wanted to erect a statue at the entrance of the great canal. He came to America for the unveiling of Liberty, taking away some of the limelight from Bartholdi.

As Liberty was getting closer to completion Henry F. Gillig, a wealthy American resident of Paris, gave a great dinner in Bartholdi's honor at the Hotel Continental on May 21, 1884. Only men were invited, as was frequently the custom in those days. The ballroom of the hotel was decorated with French and American flags "interspersed with the armorial of Alsace, of which province M. Bartholdi is a native." On the menu was an embossed reproduction of Liberty. The speeches made at this dinner were all printed in a booklet. Gillig said that Bartholdi's name "has become a household name in my own country." This was extolling the sculptor too much at that time. On the other hand the artist was too modest when he said, referring to Laboulaye, Henri Martin, and Oscar de Lafayette who were no longer alive:

I was but the modest instrument of these great minds, and if I had the merit of being persevering and courageous in the task, it was thanks to their inspiration which never abandoned me.[34]

78

Ferdinand de Lesseps also spoke and said that he expected the Panama Canal to be ready in four years, an enormous miscalculation. The Panama Canal Scandal was, however, to occur only later in the decade and could not be foreseen when he spoke. A number of toasts were proposed. It was also announced that a smaller Statue of Liberty, presented by the American residents of Paris, would be erected on a bridge or on a square. This statue now stands on the Bridge of Grenelle, in the western part of Paris.

In the course of the evening Senator Bozérian, a vice president of the *Union Franco-Américaine,* rose and narrated the following interesting anecdote:

This statue is a great work, from the point of view of art, and a colossal work from a patriotic standpoint — and yet it is something more, which perhaps you do not know: it is a work of filial piety. I will explain. (cheers) You know the artist; you know the patriot; and you will now know him as a son. A few years ago I had the honor of making his acquaintance. If I have one regret it is that this acquaintance was not made earlier. On that day, when I, with many others, commenced to harness myself to the success of our work which is finished so joyously and so well, Mr. Bartholdi said to me: "Come with me to the Opera, you will see why we are going." I accepted, and entered a dark stage box. In the corner was a lady of imposing appearance. Finding myself near Bartholdi, I said to him: "That's the Statue of Liberty!" He pressed my hand, saying: "Yes, it is." Do you know who that lady was? It was Bartholdi's mother! (cheers) Thanks to this statue, which is to be placed in the bay mentioned, the day when Bartholdi is claimed by posterity — and he is sure to be — Madame Bartholdi, his mother, will be also. (cheers) It is she in all the spendor of youth and beauty! (cheers) Was I right in telling you, gentlemen, that while describing his many qualities an important one had been forgotten, viz., that of a son? (cheers) You will join me, I am sure, in drinking a toast to Monsieur Bartholdi because of his filial piety. (cheers) [35]

Earlier in this book the author mentioned Madame Bartholdi's portrait by Ary Scheffer, hanging in one of the rooms of the *Musée Bartholdi* in Colmar. There is no doubt that the lady's appearance is imposing, although she was, when she sat for her portrait, much younger than when Senator Bozérian met her for the first time at the Opera.

Liberty was now towering high above the roofs of the houses surrounding the yard at 25 Chazelles Street, and could be seen from

quite a distance. She was still copper-colored. The greenish patina
was to come later on, after prolonged exposure to air. More and more
people came to visit her. To view the Statue one had only to ring
the bell of the janitor of the workshop. The buying of a view of the
monument, sold by the Committee to cover expenses, entitled one
to an admission ticket. The black and white view cost 50 centimes,
and enabled the viewer to visit the Statue on Thursdays and on
Sundays; the color view, costing one franc, admitted the visitor every
day of the week. The sight of Liberty awakened a variety of feelings
in the minds of those who saw her. Some would have liked to see her
placed on a summit of the Vosges, facing Germany, as a reply to the
Germania recently unveiled by the German emperor, as a symbol
that France had not given up hope of regaining Alsace some day.
Some called it "a work unique in the world which appears to our
meditations as the cathedral of modern times."[36] Others called it the
eighth marvel of the world.[37]

The date of the official presentation of the Statue of Liberty to the
Government of the United States was finally decided — July 4, 1884.
Preparations for this long expected event went ahead, and a few
days before, on June 28, Levi P. Morton, Minister Plenipotentiary
of the United States in France, who had been unable to attend the
affair of May 21 at the Hotel Continental, was the host at a great
dinner. For the July 4 event the yard in which the Statue stood was
appropriately decorated with French and American banners, some
of them at the tops of long poles. A platform with a canopy was
erected for the speakers and Liberty's torch was beflagged. The
proceedings started at 11 AM, and were over by noon. The guests
numbered about two hundred, many of them Americans living in
Paris. The presentation of the Statue in the name of the French
people was made by Ferdinand de Lesseps, the new president of the
Union Franco-Américaine, and it was received in the name of the
United States by Morton. Jules Ferry, who was French premier at
that time, had asked to be excused on account of illness, but he had
signed the official remittance document ahead of time, and had
promised free transportation for the Statue to the United States.
Jules Ferry's letter was read by Ferdinand de Lesseps, who could not
help making a reference to the Panama Canal in the speech that he
gave later. He thanked Bartholdi and his co-workers of the firm

Gaget-Gauthier, who had constructed the Statue. He concluded his speech in this manner:

This work, Mr. Minister, is the product of enthusiasm, of devotion, of intelligence, and of the noblest sentiments which can animate man. It is great in its conception and in its realization. It is colossal in its proportions, and we hope that it will grow still greater through its moral value, thanks to the remembrances and the sentiments which it is to perpetuate. We commit it to your care, Mr. Minister, that it may remain forever the pledge of the bonds which should unite France and the great American nation.[38]

Mr. Morton replied first by reading a telegram of congratulations from the President of the United States, who was at that time Chester A. Arthur. Then he praised Bartholdi and those who had helped him, and thanked France for this new testimony of friendship.

The deed for the gift was on a magnificent parchment contained in a case which was described as a marvellous specimen of the French goldsmith's art. During the ceremony a band played the French and the American national anthems, as well as the "Hail Columbia."[39] After the ceremony refreshments were served in the offices of the Gaget-Gauthier firm. This was followed by a luncheon in honor of Morton and some twenty guests, including Bartholdi, and at 5 PM there was a reception at the United States legation. On account of the great heat on that day, a smaller number of people than expected went there. Strangely enough this ceremony of Franco-American friendship was not given much prominence in the French press which, on the other hand, alloted much space to a cholera epidemic which was raging at that time. An American comment, however, was: "Americans who were so fortunate as to be in Paris on the 4th of July, 1884 witnessed perhaps the most notable celebration of the day that has ever been held in the Old World."[40] Until recently there was no plaque or marker at 25 Chazelles Street to remind the passer-by that Liberty had been constructed there. Lately, however, this omission was corrected by a gift from Milt Forrest of Hollywood, California, of a plaque riveted next to the gate of what was "the birthplace of the Statue of Liberty."[41]

CHAPTER SIX

"The World's" Campaign for the Bartholdi Pedestal Gets Under Way

It had been originally planned to disassemble the Statue of Liberty for shipment to the United States starting August 20, but this was postponed allegedly because according to the estimated length of the operation the Statue would arrive in America in the middle of winter. Besides, it has already been pointed out that the Pedestal was far from ready to receive Liberty. So Paris was allowed to keep the gigantic statue a little longer. It was to receive many more visitors, including such distinguished ones as Jules Grévy, President of the French Republic, and Victor Hugo, the famous writer. The French President was very enthusiastic. He shook hands and congratulated everyone for having completed such "an extraordinary work, the conception of which is as large and as noble as the form, and which will magnify France beyond the seas."[1]

The announced visit of Victor Hugo was to stir Bartholdi and his entourage. This visit seemed to have given the artist much more pride than that of President Grévy. Hugo was eighty-two at that time and was one of the most famous literary personalities in the world. The day before the visit Bartholdi had a little piece of copper, the same as the Statue was made of, engraved with the date of the visit, November 29, 1884, and the visitor's name, who was designated as "the illustrious apostle of Peace, Liberty and Progress." The souvenir was placed in a small case. Victor Hugo came with his grand-daughter Jeanne whom he had often pictured in his poems, and another lady, Madame Lockroy, the wife of a French play-wright. The mother and the wife of the artist were there. Bartholdi's mother was one year older than Victor Hugo, who kissed the lady's hand as he entered a room decorated with French and American flags and located near the base of the Statue. The great writer walked hatless in front of the workers forming a cluster and reached the entrance to the Statue. "It is superb!" he exclaimed, after examining a diorama showing how Liberty would look in New York harbor. Then he went up the stairs inside the Statue, and he would have climbed all the way into the head had he not been prevented from doing so because it was feared that it would be too much of a strain for the old gentleman. Before leaving, the writer remained silent for a moment looking at the Statue, then he said a few sentences that Bartholdi and his companions were to remember for a long time, concluding with these words:

Yes, this beautiful work aims at what I have always loved, called for: peace between America and France — France which is Europe — this pledge of peace will be permanent. It was a good thing that this should have been done.[2]

These were not Hugo's last words about Liberty. The following year, shortly before his death, he scribbled a few words which have been translated as follows:

To Mr. Bartholdi, May 13, 1885

Form to the sculptor is all and yet nothing. It is nothing without the spirit: with the idea it is everything.

Victor Hugo[3]

In January 1885 the Statue was closed to the public so that dis-assembling of the huge figure might start. This was a tremendous job as all parts had to be numbered and crated. The French share of the project was about to be completed. It was now America's turn to give Liberty a place to stand upon.

The Pedestal situation looked very distressing early in 1885, when Liberty was being readied for her trip to the United States. On

March 12 of that year Spaulding, the treasurer of the American Committee on the Statue of Liberty, presented a report at a meeting in the Bryant Building, at the corner of Liberty and Nassau Streets, New York City. That report stated that between December 1, 1884 and March 10, 1885 only $15,662.19 had been received, and that the total received from the time of the opening of the fund-raising campaign amounted to $182,491.40. It will be remembered that the total reached on November 10, 1884, according to the subscription booklet, was $161,489.85.[4] Money was therefore coming in, but too slowly to keep up with the progress of the work and the coming in of the bills which had to be paid. The treasurer's report said that of the $182,491.40 collected, $179,624.51 had already been spent, leaving a balance of $2,866.89 in the Committee's treasury. More than ninety per cent of the money contributed had come from New York City and its immediate vicinity. Now, the Statue of Liberty was about to be shipped to the United States, and at the rate the money was coming in it would take years to complete the Pedestal. What could be done? No doubt a turning point had been reached. The Committee had tried all possible means to raise money: a request for an appropriation from Congress had not been successful; neither had *The World's* campaign of 1883 given any worthwhile results; a tour by an "agitator" through the West in order to arouse interest in the project had not brought in much money. Most people felt that since the Statue of Liberty was to be erected in New York harbor it was up to New Yorkers, or at least to the people living nearby, to raise the necessary money to give Liberty a footstool.

This is what the situation looked like in March 1885. Work on the foundations of the Pedestal had started as soon as the first money had come in, under the direction of General Stone, chief engineer, assisted by Hunt, chief architect. The work had followed its course more or less regularly until May 1884, when the foundations were completed. On August 5 of that same year, one month after the presentation of the Statue of Liberty to the United States in Paris, the cornerstone of the Pedestal had been laid, amidst impressive ceremonies. The monument had a stormy beginning; it rained and thundered during most of the proceedings. The cornerstone was a beautiful six-ton granite block from Leete, Connecticut. Among the various objects and documents which were placed in the copper

84

casket inserted in the stone was an old silver 50-cent coin, struck in the year 1824, the year when Lafayette visited the United States. The cornerstone laying, which took place shortly after 2 PM, was a ceremony masonic in character with General Stone wearing Egyptian orders.[5] It may be mentioned in this connection that Bartholdi was also a mason. Many of the 750 invitations to the ceremony sent out by the American Committee on the Statue of Liberty had been answered with letters of regret, many prominent people having already left New York for the summer. A French newspaper reporting the proceedings wrote that another $125,000 was needed to complete the work, but that there was no doubt that the amount would be obtained. It was only a matter of time.[6] The Committee had hoped that the laying of the cornerstone, with the publicity surrounding it, would give an impetus to subscriptions. However, a short time after this event work on the Pedestal had been suspended altogether.

Favorable publicity would certainly have made a difference. However, throughout the campaign a number of newspapers had allowed publication of articles highly critical of the whole project. They were to get on the bandwagon only towards the end and join in the praise of Liberty. An example of the critical articles written when the Statue project was only in its infancy has already been given.[7] Here is another which appeared in a respectable newspaper under the title of "Looking at a Gift Horse in the Mouth."

The painful parsimony of the Frenchmen who have undertaken to present this city with the statue of "Liberty Enlightening the World" is simply disgusting. They have, in effect, told us that we cannot have the statue unless we provide it with a pedestal. This effort to compel us to pay out of our own money for the embellishment of our harbor has not yet been condemned by the press with the severity it deserves.[8]

The article continued in the same ironical tone, referring to the Frenchmen's attempt upon "our pockets," and to their taking advantage of "our fondness for big things." The writer of the article added that the Statue could not well be refused because it could "at any time be broken up and sold for old metal for a considerable sum." The French, the article continued, had underestimated "our shrewdness as a commercial people" because it had been established that the Pedestal would cost more than the Statue would bring in if

85

sold for scrap. The writer of this article then suggested that the French erect the Statue themselves and pay $10,000 a year as rent for the site.

Bartholdi read this article, which was sent to him by the *Argus* newspaper clipping agency, and placed it in his files. His work, however, was just about finished, and he could take such irony much better than in 1876, when a newspaper editorial aroused him to write a reply. The editorial concerned the Statue which was in the process of being made, while the article mentioned above had to do with the Pedestal. This was America's part in the project. People reading articles ridiculing the Statue of Liberty campaign were not very likely to send money to the Committee, and therefore it was not surprising that money was hard to come by.

In March 1885 when the situation looked rather hopeless there remained about 75 more feet of solid granite work to be erected in order to complete the Pedestal. Hearing of New York's predicament, cities all over the United States, such as Boston, Cleveland, and San Francisco, offered a home to Liberty, claiming they could get the money for a pedestal in no time. It has already been pointed out that Philadelphia would have liked to have had it for its Fairmount Park right at the start. After surveying this distressing situation the American Committee on the Statue of Liberty figured that about $100,000 would be needed to complete the job, and decided to launch a last and desperate appeal to the public. Here is an abstract of this stirring appeal:

If the money is not forthcoming the statue must return to its donors to the everlasting disgrace of the American people, or it must go to some other city to the everlasting disgrace of New York. Citizens of the State, citizens of the metropolis, we ask you once for all to prevent so painful and humiliating a catastrophe![9]

The appeal was signed by William Evarts, Richard Butler, and Henry Spaulding.

In spite of the failure of his 1883 subscription campaign in *The World,* Joseph Pulitzer accepted the challenge to raise the $100,000. This time he was determined not to give up until the final goal was reached. In between these two campaigns *The World* had assumed stature. It had campaigned with success for the candidacy of Grover Cleveland, who had been elected to the presidency of the United States in 1884 on the Democrat ticket. Pulitzer had gained success and increased his paper's circulation from a few thousands copies to over one hundred thousand by emphasizing sensational news and using political cartoons. *The World* was considered by many as "the people's newspaper." Pulitzer was therefore in a better position to help Liberty in 1885 than he had been in 1883, but even so it was to be rough going in face of the indifference and even hostility of many people.

On March 16, 1885 Pulitzer made his famous appeal to the American public, from which the following passages are taken:

Money must be raised to complete the pedestal for the Bartholdi Statue. It would be an ineffaceable disgrace to New York City and the American Republic to have France send this splendid gift without our having provided even so much as a landing place for it. . . The statue is now completed and ready to be brought to our shores in a vessel especially commissioned by the French Government. Congress, by a refusal to appropriate the necessary money to complete preparations for its proper reception and erection, has thrown the responsibility back to the American people. . . The two hundred and fifty thousand dollars that the making of the statue cost was paid in by the masses of the French people — by the working men, the tradesmen, the shopgirls, the artisans — by all, irrespective of class or condition. Let us respond in like manner. Let us not wait for the millionaires to give the money. . . Take this appeal to yourself personally. It is meant for every reader of *THE WORLD*. Give something, however little. Send it to us. We will receive it, and see that it is properly applied. We will also publish the name of every giver, however small the sum given. Let us hear from the people.[10]

Day after day the newspaper published editorials encouraging the people to give. The response was immediate. The very next day after the publication of the appeal *The World* started printing amounts, names, and some letters. Subscription blanks were made available to groups, and people were cautioned not to give to unauthorized persons. Among the first to give was the Hotel Men's Relief Society that sent $232. Most subscriptions, however, were much smaller and were usually accompanied by letters such as this one:

I am a young man of foreign birth and have seen enough of monarchical government to appreciate the blessings of this Republic. Enclosed please find two dollars for the Bartholdi Fund.

Nathan Fleisch, Orange, New Jersey
March 17[11]

In the March 18 editorial *The World* proposed to make just such a fight for the Bartholdi Statue Pedestal as it had made for Cleveland. "Cleveland was elected and the Pedestal will be erected." A first prize consisting of two double Eagles (forty dollars in gold) was promised to the person who would send in the largest amount of money. Among the suggestions made early in the subscription campaign was this one: let every reader of *The World* give 25 cents and get his friends to do likewise, and the amount will be obtained within a week with a surplus.

Occasionally the paper published comments from out-of-town newspapers, such as this one from the *Troy Times* in up-state New York. "Perhaps the country was not perishing for a statue of Liberty, but now that it is tendered we should not act like a nation of untamed cowboys in regard to it."[12] The *Boston Daily Advertiser* had this sarcastic comment:

It is certainly better that the money should be collected in this way than not at all. But it is not particularly creditable to a city as rich and as boastful as New York that it should have to beg for the funds through the public press.[13]

The larger New York papers, which did not think too much of the Statue of Liberty at that time, naturally cared very little about the appeal made by *The World*. This paper once quoted a comment which appeared in the *New York Tribune* on March 19, 1885: "It is a pretty cold day when *The World* doesn't get at least 13 cents for the Bartholdi Statue Pedestal."[14] *The World* suggested that the *Tribune* join it in raising money, but this suggestion, of course, was disregarded. Should Liberty ever be damaged, newspapers all over the country, especially in New York, would rise to the occasion. But in 1885 it was mainly *The World's* concern that Liberty should find a home on these shores.

It is probable that one of the main reasons why the leading newspapers were not sympathetic to *The World's* efforts was because they were largely controlled by wealthy people, and such people were constantly taunted by this newspaper on account of their lack of support. The Goulds, the Vanderbilts, and others were repeatedly taken to task instead of being left alone. On March 19, for instance, the paper announced that a $500 Confederate note had been sent in by William H. Vanderbilt and Jay Gould. The letters which were published often had disparaging references to the rich, such as this one:

A few poor fellows, whose pockets are not as deep as a well, but whose love for liberty is wider than a church door, hand you the enclosed $7.25 as their mite towards the Bartholdi Pedestal Fund. May Heaven help you in your good work; it seems that New York's rich men do not.[15]

On March 21 *The World* wrote that the Germans had raised $750,000 for Bismarck's seventieth birthday, while the Americans could not scrape up one third of this sum for Liberty. As the same time, however, an editorial expressed confidence that the public would respond when they knew the need, and it pointed out the growing interest in the campaign. "*The World* does not mean to stop till the splendid gift of the French people is firmly fixed upon a substantial resting place," the editorial of March 21 proclaimed. It went on saying: "There shall be a place for Liberty to set her feet. Take heed of this all ye croakers and laggards!" A letter appearing in the same issue of the newspaper suggested that the Democrats should build the Pedestal to celebrate their victory at the polls. By March 22 the Bartholdi Pedestal Fund of *The World* had reached $2,172.52, including the $1,000 subscribed by the paper itself and money gathered during the earlier campaign, that of 1883. It was still very little, but it was a beginning. After all, the fund-raising campaign had not yet lasted a whole week.

People were sending money they had saved in various ways. Here is what Jimmy Palmer wrote about what he had done:

Since leaving smoking cigarettes I have gained twenty-five pounds, so I cheerfully enclose a penny for each pound. Having increased my own stature, I donate this to the Statue of Liberty. I also feel improved mentally and I am trying to induce others to abandon this pernicious practice.[16]

Children as well as adults were trying to help:

I am a little girl, nine years old, and I would like to do something for the Statue Fund. I will send you a pair of my pet game bantams, if you will sell them and give the money to the Statue.

Florence de Foreest
Metuchen, New Jersey[17]

The newspaper commended the little girl for her letter, and later, after the arrival of the birds at the newspaper office, news about how they were faring was given now and again until they finally found a new owner.

Meanwhile the American Committee on the Statue of Liberty was not inactive; it was not relying on *The World* to do all the work. On March 24 the newspaper published an "Appeal to Patriotism" from the Committee. This appeal was reprinted frequently. It does not make any reference to *The World's* campaign, maybe in order not to antagonize any possible rich donors. The fact, however, that *The World* was asked to print it could be considered as an endorsement of its campaign. As on previous occasions there was a picture of Uncle Sam holding a hat near a globe. This time there was also a letter from five-year-old Herni, Second Avenue, Astoria, New York: "Please put the enclosed (60 cents) into the old man's hat, for I love him too much to see him beg."

The World's announcement that the "Bartholdi Statue" would arrive about May 1 aroused some other newspapers to offer to receive money and send it to Joseph Pulitzer's newspaper. Among these was the *Buffalo Times* from up-state New York. Such offers were to become more numerous later on as the campaign became more successful, as if other newspapers were afraid of being left behind. Such offers were to come also from out-of-state papers. Meanwhile, however, a newspaper from Columbus, Ohio, was reported to have written about *The World's* campaign that the responsibility of raising money lay on New York alone and that attempts to create interest elsewhere would fail.[18] On the same day as this comment was printed the New York newspaper referred to the Lafayette statue in Union Square, New York, the pedestal of which was a gift from the city's French residents and wrote: "and now the French people have given us a grander statue by the same artist of Liberty herself."

Looking through successive issues of *The World,* one cannot help being surprised at Joseph Pulitzer's and his staff's resourcefulness at keeping up the public's interest in the campaign by various devices — now flattering, now rebuking; opposing the poor to the rich; often printing cartoons, one of which appears in this book. Considering all the problems involved this was really a tough job, and one cannot help feeling that not only Bartholdi should be remembered more than he now is, but also Pulitzer.

On March 27 the Bartholdi Statue Pedestal Fund had reached the sum of $3,359.67, all of which was provided by 2,535 persons with the exception of the $1,000 given by *The World.* The smallest single subscription was 5 cents, which had been sent in the day before the announcement, by Joseph R. Ryon, of 26 South Street, New York, an office boy. The ultimate goal of $100,000 was still a long way off, but the American Committee was continuing to receive contributions. On the same day a list of contributors to the Committee's Fund was also published which included seven who had given one hundred dollars each. This made a total sum of $1,105.49. No doubt *The World's* campaign was arousing some people to give more generously, and the fact that the Committee was still receiving money made it possible for people who would not condescend to be associated with *The World's* pennies and dimes givers to send in larger amounts of money. However, *The World* had set for itself the goal of raising the $100,000 and was going to do it regardless of the amounts the American Committee on the Statue of Liberty was to raise. As time went on, more people who were able to subscribe large amounts sent them to *The World.* The lists of contributors were becoming longer and longer as days went by. There were occasionally spelling mistakes and errors in amounts, which were unavoidable and which were always rectified on request. It was quite a job to handle all these letters and small amounts of money day after day and meet the printing deadline.

Interest in *The World's* campaign was increasing, and this interest took various forms. Benefit performances were given to raise money, such as that given by the *Columbia Maennerchor,* a German singing ensemble which announced a concert at Steinway Hall on May 3.

One person, instead of mailing money to *The World,* sent in a Japanese goatskin baby carriage robe to be sold for the fund. It was promptly bought by Pulitzer who had use for it. The *Chillicothe Advertiser* claimed if the Statue of Liberty was sent to illuminate the Ohio-Erie Canal money for a pedestal would be raised in twenty-four hours.[19] In its editorial of the last day of March, two weeks after the beginning of the fund-raising campaign, Pulitzer's paper recalled that the memorial to the Scottish poet Burns in Westminster Abbey, London, had been erected with small subscriptions from Scotland. Liberty's Pedestal should be the People's Pedestal. Every visitor to New York will want to see the Statue of Liberty. This the people can bring about, the paper added, with their dollars and dimes. All this was done to encourage and to taunt people into making contributions. As to the prediction that every visitor to New York would want to see the Statue of Liberty, *The World* was correct. Bartholdi's monument is still attracting hundreds of thousands of visitors every year, especially during the summer season. On returns from trips to Europe, this writer has often seen visitors rising early in the morning to go on the deck of the liner to have their first view of New York. What were they particularly anxious to see? The Empire State Building? The United Nations? No, the Statue of Liberty of which they had seen so many pictures before coming to this country.

On April 1 the announcement, of course premature, that Liberty would leave France about May 8 prompted Pierre Lorillard, the descendant of a French Huguenot who had founded America's oldest tobacco company in 1760, to give $1,000. The Lorillard firm was located in Jersey City, New Jersey, at the time of this gift. Frank Siddall[20] of Philadelphia started sending in one dollar a day with the promise not to stop doing this until the goal was reached. He was to do this for 133 days. On April 14 the editorial addressed an appeal to William H. Vanderbilt, whose income was reported to be $1,250 an hour, and the following day another appeal was addressed to Jay Gould, whose income was supposed to be $500 an hour. These were naturally jokes since nothing was expected for Liberty from such quarters, but they served the purpose of keeping alive interest in the campaign. People were always looking forward to see what *The World* would bring up the next day.

Early in the month of April the attitude of the other New York newspapers started to change. *The World's* campaign might succeed after all, they probably figured. Congratulations from the *New York Tribune* were published and *The World* tried to take advantage of this to renew its request to the *Tribune* and to other papers in general to help with the campaign, but this was going a little too fast. It was also suggested that churches might help on Easter Sunday by taking a collection for the fund, the paper added that "Patriotism and Religion" could go together.[21] This author has not found any record that any church in New York had taken up a collection for Liberty on Easter Sunday 1885; churches were to become interested in the project only later on.

It was also early in April 1885 that the announcement was made of the opening at the *Eden Musee,* New York, which no longer exists, of an historical display of all the presidents of the United States in life-size figures surrounding Bartholdi's Statue of Liberty. Admission for adults was to be 50 cents. The *Casino* on Broadway and 89th Street gave "a monster entertainment" to aid the Pedestal Fund, which yielded $1,400.

The Statue of Liberty also inspired poets and *The World* occasionally printed poems. The best-known poem connected with the Statue of Liberty, however, was written in 1883. It was "The New Colossus" by Emma Lazarus from New York. Here it is:

Not like the brazen giant of Greek fame,
With conquering limbs astride from land to land;
Here at our sea-washed, sunset gates shall stand
A mighty woman with a torch, whose flame
Is the imprisoned lightning, and her name
Mother of Exiles. From her beacon-hand
Glows world-wide welcome; her mild eyes command
The air-bridged harbor that twin cities frame.
"Keep ancient lands, your storied pomp!" cries she
With silent lips. "Give me your tired, your poor,
Your huddled masses yearning to breathe free,
The wretched refuse of your teeming shore.
Send these, the homeless, tempest-tost to me,
I lift my lamp beside the golden door!"

Verses from this poem are sometimes found on the back of postcards representing Liberty, but they are not engraved on the Statue as some people think. They are engraved on a plaque located below the Statue in the hall that leads to the stairs and elevator. The prominence given to that poem over all the others is probably to be attributed to three main reasons.

First, the feelings expressed appealed to many people. The representation of Liberty as the "Mother of Exiles" touched the hearts of the many immigrants who were waiting at Ellis Island for clearance of their immigration status and were seeing Liberty close-by. It should be added, however, that such feelings are also found in other poems, as will be seen in the course of this work, although no other poem will be given in full. One of them called "Liberty Enlightening the World," written by C. P. Schermerhorn, had as many as twenty-one stanzas of four lines each. This was the longest one that this author has come across.

Second, the fact that Emma Lazarus was Jewish and born in New York, appealed to the many Jews who came to this country towards the end of the last century and to the large number of Jews living in New York. But this is not reason enough, as Pulitzer, who was also a Jew, did a great deal for the Statue of Liberty, and is not well remembered in this connection.

A third factor which was probably very important was that Liberty is embodied by a woman, that Emma Lazarus was a woman, and that for a number of years the organization which has been sponsoring ceremonies at the Statue of Liberty has been The Ladies Auxiliary of Veterans of Foreign Wars of the United States. There is no doubt that the publicity given to Emma Lazarus' poem has contributed a great deal to making the Statue of Liberty the great symbol it now is, and a Statue whose features are familiar to millions all over the world.

On April 3 *The World* published its first little poem as part of the 1885 campaign. It was very short, without any author's name, and called "Better Chip In." On the 5th came a longer one by Harry Kennedy, a national anthem entitled "Liberty." This poem had not been written especially for the campaign, as the copyright is from the previous year. However, it was announced that the poem would be sold with the music at 50 cents a copy for the benefit of the Pedestal. Each of the stanzas ends with the word "Liberty."

The day after the printing of Kennedy's poem Pulitzer's newspaper struck upon the idea of appealing to wealthy widows. Their names were printed, as well as estimates of their fortunes. Those women, the paper wrote, should know that "Madame Liberty is without a resting place." At the same time there was the recurrent nagging of millionaires who perhaps "as a rule have no affection for Liberty. But poor people have."[22] Needless to say that none of the widows came forward to help build up the Pedestal Fund. However, the listing of their estimated fortunes added some interest to the campaign. People who do not have much are only too anxious to know about wealthy families' affairs. The *Herald* of Chicago, while praising *The World's* effort, suggested that if the campaign did not succeed the Statue should go to the city which would take care of it. Thus adding indirectly Chicago to the list of cities which would have liked to have Liberty. There were, however, indications that New York was going to have it and that the fund-raising campaign was encouraging people in the right places. The executive committee of the American Committee on the Statue of Liberty, under the chairmanship of Drexel, authorized the resumption of the quarrying and cutting of stone for the Pedestal. In one single day $2,044.98 came in at *The World's* offices, including $606 from members of the watch and jewelry trade. Each of them had donated one dollar and the names were on a twenty-five-foot scroll. *The World* fitted them all in one column, four abreast. The editorial of April 9 suggested that the rule forbidding the collection of money from school children should be suspended for the cause of the Statue. As a precedent the paper quoted Secretary Manning who had allowed subscription blanks to circulate in the Treasury Department, although it was against the rules. It has been mentioned that artists were not keen about the Statue of Liberty, so the newspaper took them to task for not giving anything, referring to the smaller replica of Liberty about to be erected in Paris, one of the world's leading art centers.

Meanwhile money was continuing to come in; more names and more letters were being printed, such as this one:

I see by the paper this morning that a little boy, one year old, contributed one dollar to the Pedestal Fund. Although I cannot creep I can shout for the cause of Liberty when my papa and my mama want to sleep. Enclosed please find one dollar from a little boy eight months old.

Sumner D. Aspinwall, Jr.
Newark, New Jersey, April 8[23]

A Blaine man, having waited for some time for the *New York Tribune* to do something about the Statue so that he could subscribe through a Republican paper, made up his mind to send in one dollar. The *Post Dispatch* of Saint Louis, which Pulitzer had run before acquiring *The World* and still owned, started to raise money, and subscriptions were started in other cities. A box placed in the bar of Hoffman House, an important New York hotel, yielded $10.21. Boxes were placed elsewhere; usually not only coins, but buttons and other items were found when they were opened.

Finally, on April 15 the sum of $25,762.36 was on hand, a little over a quarter of the total sought, and on April 17 *The World* proudly sent its first $25,000 check to the American Committee on the Statue of Liberty. This amount had been collected in one month only. The money had been coming in stamps, pennies, nickels, dimes, postal orders, bills, silver, and gold. The handling of this had been a painstaking task. Very little had been lost. The money had to be counted every single day to make it possible to acknowledge the gifts. Occasionally complaints had been received that some amounts had not been acknowledged, but this had always been rectified. It has already been mentioned that typographical errors had been unavoidable and had always been rectified whenever brought to the attention of the newspaper staff. A few forged checks were sent in, but the names with the amounts were printed in order to discourage this practice. One month later another $25,000 was available. With half the total amount of $100,000 obtained in only two months the campaign was proving a success. The collection of the second $50,000 was to take a little longer — nearly three months — but various circumstances, especially the arrival of the Statue of Liberty in New York, did not leave a shadow of doubt that the $100,000 would be obtained. The most difficult part of the campaign was over.

CHAPTER SEVEN

The Arrival of the Statue of Liberty in the United States and the Success of "The World's" Fund-Raising Campaign

About the time *The World* remitted the first $25,000 to the American Committee on the Statue of Liberty, the secretary of this organization, Richard Butler, received a letter from the *Union Franco-Américaine* in Paris, signed by Auguste Bartholdi, announcing that the dismantling of the Statue of Liberty was proceeding according to schedule and that the Statue would leave about May 4. This also was to prove too early, and it was just as well for the Pedestal engineer, because in May the Pedestal was just about rising again. The letter added that there were customs formalities to clear for the Statue. "We hope," Bartholdi wrote, "that you will soon attain complete success on your side, and that the arrival of the Statue will contribute to this end."[1] Meanwhile plans were going ahead for the erection of Liberty in Paris, a gift of the United States residents of the French capital. This statue was to be exactly the same size as the final model of the Statue of Liberty which had been divided into sections to be enlarged four times in order to obtain the final dimensions of the great Statue now in New York harbor. It was to be placed on the Square of the United States, and was to be unveiled in the middle of May 1885, at the time of a farewell dinner given to Levi P. Morton who was leaving his post to return to the United States. The Paris Liberty, however, did not stay at the place where it was unveiled, and it has already been mentioned that it now stands on the Bridge of Grenelle over the Seine River. The plaque which has been put on it has an inscription which indicates that is was definitively erected there only in 1889. On the plaque is also an extract from a letter from Morton, who by that time had become vice president of the United States. The first two sentences of this letter translated from the French read as follows:

We venerate the France of the past because her soldiers have helped us become a nation; and we like the France of today because she has united herself with us in the cause of free governments.

The second phase of the fund-raising campaign of *The World* witnessed a "nationalization" of the Statue of Liberty project, with contributions now coming not only from the New York area but from all over the United States. *The World* quoted the Philadelphia *Daily News,* which wrote that the Statue of Liberty did not belong to New York alone but that it belonged to the whole country.[2] This was certainly an encouraging change which foretold the final success of the campaign. Now, it appeared that New York would get the Statue after all, so it would belong to all. There was no doubt some envy, especially on the part of Philadelphia. The inhabitants of that city would have liked to have had Liberty all the time and had hoped that New York would not be able to raise the money for the Pedestal, as is shown by the following spiteful comment which appeared in the *Philadelphia Bulletin:*

If the New York *World* goes on raising money at this rate for the Bartholdi Pedestal, it will soon become an open question whether New York shall not put Mr. Pulitzer's statue on the pedestal instead of Bartholdi's Liberty. New York would not know the difference.[3]

On Sunday, April 26 *The World* published interviews with artists, as if enough was not known already about what they thought of Liberty. As was to be expected most of them were noncommittal and said they wanted to wait and see how it looked once it stood in the harbor. Saint Gaudens, whose address was given at West 36th Street, New York, said that he looked at Liberty primarily as a national project and hoped that it would be successful. The Philadelphia Sketch Club mailed ten dollars in the hope of stimulating the in-

Merchants Street in Colmar. Bartholdi was born in 1834
in a house located a little further up on this street.

Bartholdi's birth and death are commemorated in Colmar (1954)

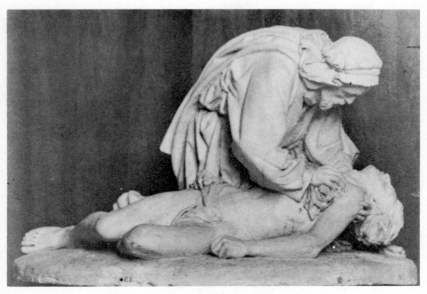

The Good Samaritan. The first work by Bartholdi to be exhibited in a *Salon* in Paris.

Bartholdi and his mother.

The music room in the *Musée Bartholdi* in Colmar, artist's former home.

Lighthouse planned for Suez — Presented to Khedive 1869.

Statue of Liberty's arm in New York.

Statue of Liberty's head in Paris.

Artist's wife.

104

Artist's mother.

Bartholdi in his studio in Paris.

Le roi des quincailliers est sur le premier plan,
Dietz-Monnin; au second, monsieur de Talleyrand.

Caricature from Bartholdi's *Album du Bord*.
(The king of the ironmongers
is in the foreground, Dietz-Monnin;
in the second, Mr. de Talleyrand).

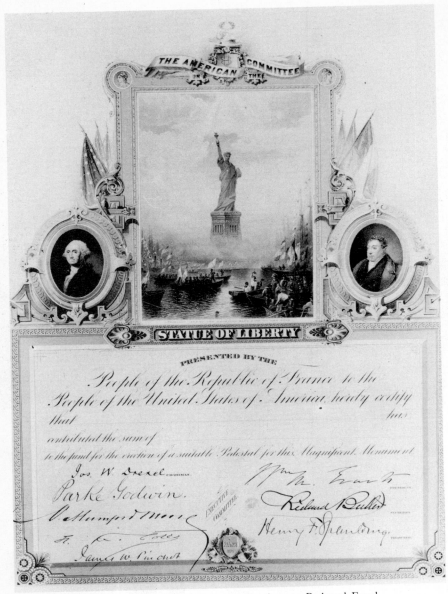

Certificate to acknowledge contributions to Pedestal Fund.

View of the workshop in which the Statue of Liberty was built in Paris.

THE UNFINISHED PEDESTAL.

WHAT SHALL BE DONE WITH THE GREAT BARTHOLDI STATUE?

Retrospect of the Work Done—Money Collected
and Money Expended—How Congress Failed
to Give $100,000—Condition and Prospects of
the Work on Bedloe's Island—The Necessity
of Immediate Action—A Liberal Contribution
from the Hotel Men.

THE PEDESTAL AS IT IS.

THUS WE HOPE TO SEE IT.

OLD ENTRANCE
TO THE FORT

Pictures published by *The World* on March 16, 1885 when
it launched its great campaign for Liberty's Pedestal.

108

World.

K, SUNDAY, APRIL 12, 1885---TWENTY-FOUR PAGES.

A New
ton Ba
calcula
the Sp
THE
hypoth

cipally as can be

t there is great
his is manifested
o by other troops
ttailors of Coe
The garrison at
ay in hastening
that point, and
their full capa-
ions.

RETIRE.

e War Minister
nda.

he war feeling
. The Czar ap-
g. The audience
rs from Penjdeh
Komaroff's con-
al-arms when
o building with

members of the
this evening at
r the benefit of
e of the Czar
. The National
audience, and
ront of his box
ated with a tur-
was continued
party was fol-
he gates of the

g to a circle of
assurance of
height advance.

speaking evi-
mments upon
s in the British
incident as
ould have been
rs to have sus-
t of more com-
have acted on
y that Russian
entions of the
t good reason.
that collisions
the Kusha are
f a violent and
The Penjdeh
s certainly an
dversely affect
en Russia and
pe for peace,
the most rabid
now predicts
Le Nord is
f the Russian
lieved to have
erto expressed
now says that
open devalr

THE MONEY KINGS AND THE STATUE OF LIBERTY.

A cartoon published by *The World* during the fund-raising campaign.

Grand Annual Reception
—OF THE—
BARTHOLDI CLUB,
on Monday Evening, Nov. 23rd, 1885,
—AT—

LYRIC HALL,

SIXTH AVENUE AND 42nd STREET.

TICKETS ADMIT GENTLEMAN AND LADY 50 CTS.

OFFICERS :

Pres. WM. GUENTHNER,   Vice Pres. JOHN B. DWYER.
Sec'y ANDREW WIELAND.   Tres. ROBERT L. HAHN.

—MUSIC BY PROFESSOR McDONALD—

The now non-existent Bartholdi Club was founded shortly before the
unveiling of the Statue of Liberty.

109

The Statue of Liberty about to be completed in Paris.

Souvenir

PROGRAMME

Of the Unveiling
to the Government:

and Presentation
of the United States

Of the Bartholdi

Conceived 1865.

Statue of Liberty

Completed 1886.

ILLUMINATED BY THE AMERICAN SYSTEM OF ELECTRIC LIGHTING

AT LIBERTY ISLAND,
New York Bay,
OCTOBER 28TH, 1886.

PRICE, 10 CENTS.

111

Published on front page of *The World* on October 28, 1886. (To put my name at the feet of great men and at the service of grand ideas, such is my ambition. A. Bartholdi).

The Parade Passing Under "The World's" Arch.

THE ORIGINAL DRAWING OF THE PEDESTAL.

FAC-SIMILE OF BARTHOLDI'S SKETCH.

THE ORIGINAL DESIGN.

The Statue of Liberty as visualized by Bartholdi, surrounded by figures of the Nation's heroes.

Ticket for a dance given by people originally from Colmar on the first anniversary of the unveiling of the Statue of Liberty.

American G.I.s looking at Bartholdi's monument in Colmar towards end of World War II.

terest of other artistic organizations.[4] Columbia College in New York City started raising money for the Pedestal, reporting the amounts each week in the *Columbia Spectator* and forwarding them to *The World*. This newspaper had an advertisement every day for the small statuettes of Liberty sold by the American Committee.

Around this time the American press — with some exceptions — started a turnabout in favor of the Statue of Liberty, and churches did likewise. There had been some opposition on the part of clergymen to Liberty because the Statue's appearance reminded them of a pagan goddess, and they did not think it proper that such a monument should stand at the gate of Christian America. It has been previously mentioned that Pulitzer's appeal to churches to take a collection on Easter Sunday for the Bartholdi Pedestal had met with no response — as far as the author knows. In May 1885 the Reverend H. H. Barbour of the North Baptist Church in Philadelphia announced that a collection for the Pedestal would be taken on Sunday, May 31. He suggested that other churches should do likewise and that Decoration Day would be "a particularly appropriate occasion to appreciate liberty which enables people to worship in perfect freedom."[5] From then on more and more references are found regarding the interest of religious bodies in the Statue of Liberty and in *The World's* campaign in particular. For instance, $16.88 was sent in by Rabbi F. de Sola Mendes of the synagogue located at West 44th Street and 6th Avenue, New York. The money came from the children's classes.[6]

Bartholdi himself took part in the fund-raising campaign through the publication, under his name, of a sixty-six-page book, richly illustrated and written in English, which was entitled: *The Statue of Liberty Enlightening the World, Described by the Sculptor Bartholdi, Published for the Benefit of the Pedestal Fund by the North American Review*.[7] The material in this book, of which only a few copies are still available, was arranged in May 1885 by Allen Thorndike Rice who wrote the Preface. It contained an account by Bartholdi of how the Statue of Liberty project was conceived. It has been mentioned before that this account was meant to appeal to the general public and did not tell the whole story. Some speeches or parts of speeches delivered in France in connection with the fund-raising campaign for the Statue of Liberty were given in English translation. One section of the book concerned colossal statuary about which Bartholdi wrote:

Colossal statuary does not consist simply in making an enormous statue. It ought to produce an emotion in the breast of the spectator, not because of its volume, but because its size is in keeping with the idea that it interprets, and with the place which it ought to occupy.[8]

Bartholdi acknowledged the considerable influence of Egyptian colossal statuary on his taste for large monuments. He gave the measurements of the largest statues in existence, all of them smaller than Liberty, and told how the artist should take advantage of the natural surroundings to enhance the aspects of his monument, avoiding the neighborhood of large masses. In this connection it may be said that the location of the Statue of Liberty was well selected, because it is separated by a fairly large expanse of water from any tall building which may yet arise against the New York skyline. Bartholdi pointed out that the creator of gigantic statuary has to avoid the danger of the multiplicity of details because this would destroy the proportions of the work. Another section went into detail about the work on the Statue in the Paris workshop. Some material from this source has been used in other places in this book.

The American Committee on the Statue of Liberty finally announced that, encouraged by *The World's* support, work on the Pedestal had been resumed on May 11. The newspaper had given this news earlier, but what had actually started at that time was the cutting of stones which were to be laid on in superposed courses. Only eight out of forty-six courses were in place.

Although the Statue of Liberty was primarily meant to commemorate and strengthen the ties of friendship between France and the United States, very early it became a symbol of the United States as a haven of freedom for people fleeing from oppression abroad. This feeling which was expressed in Emma Lazarus' famous poem, which is quoted in this book, was to be found in a great many letters printed by *The World,* such as this one:

Please accept the enclosed small sum and add it to your Fund for the Bartholdi Pedestal. I could not come with my contribution before as I have been out of work, and I received today my first earnings and I am

116

able to spare ten per cent of it for Liberty's sake. I would send you more if I could, as I know how to appreciate liberty, because I am a Jew and emigrated from Russia to this city a few years ago. I think that the Germans who fled in 1848 to this country and the Jews who came here a few years ago from such countries where they have have been persecuted as Russia, Germany, Hungary and Rumania, ought to support you in your noble undertaking, as I am one of them and know my feeling. Wishing you and your great army of subscribers success, I remain yours.

A Russian Jew[9]

This letter encouraged other Jewish immigrants from Eastern Europe to send in their mites. One of them said that he was only a poor peddler, but that he was enjoying the liberty of this country. The fund-raising campaign was also starting to reach other people of foreign birth, such as the Italians. Shortly after the publication of the letter from the Russian Jew, an appeal to support the campaign appeared in *Il Progresso Italo-Americano* in New York.

The constant taunting of the rich by *The World* was criticized by the *Rochester Democrat and Chronicle*. To this the New York paper retorted that it had not been the first to do this and, besides, by not supporting the campaign the rich men of New York were making a mistake and might be branded by the masses as "enemies of liberty."[10] By May 16, 1885 a total of 53,702 people had sent in $51,070.25, and the second $25,000 installment was sent to the American Committee on the Statue of Liberty.

It was in May 1885 that *The World* received one of the largest contributions — a check for $2,000 from the Amateur Minstrel Jubilee at the Acadamy in New York, with another $200 yet to come. An unexpected support came from Colonel Knox, editor of *Texas Siftings,* who gave two lectures for the Pedestal Fund — one in New York, and the other in Philadelphia. Both drew large audiences. These lectures attracted Bartholdi's attention in France. He wrote a letter of thanks in which he said that he was gratified because Colonel Knox was from Texas. The sculptor believed that Texas was the remotest state from the Statue of Liberty. Some of New York's large establishments were following the example of the American Express Company by sending out subscription blanks to their agents. A grocer clerk of Elizabeth, New Jersey, got an afternoon off from work and went around to all grocers of the town, collecting $17.[11] Only two grocers refused to contribute to the fund. Maybe they were competitors of his boss.

A reporter for *The World* went around to see business people in order to find out what they thought of the newspaper's fund-raising campaign. While all had favorable comments, some expressed regret that Congress had failed to appropriate the money requested. This action was termed by a business man as "stinginess of which many an American will be ashamed." It ought to be mentioned in this connection that this failure to appropriate the $100,000 needed to complete the Pedestal of the Statue of Liberty had brought about unfavorable comments in the French press. Some newspapers had wondered whether the Statue should be sent to the United States where there was so little enthusiasm about providing it with a resting place. It has been explained that the request for the appropriation had been attached to a bill which did not get through. According to some sources, however, the whole thing had not been only a matter of procedure, but a rather unruly situation had prevailed in the House of Representatives when the vote was taken.[12]

The date of the departure from France of the cases containing the Statue of Liberty had been repeatedly postponed, but more and more was being published about the matter fairly often. It was known that they would be transported aboard the ship *Isère* and, at the beginning of May, the New York Chamber of Commerce appointed a committee to prepare a reception and a banquet at Delmonico's for the commander and officers of the French ship which was expected to arrive around June 20.

The crates containing the sections of the dismantled Statue were shipped from Rouen, the French inland port on the Seine, which can be reached by ocean-going vessels. It took about seventy large railroad trucks to carry the crated pieces of the Statue of Liberty and its framework from Paris to Rouen. The loading of the crates, which weighed between one hundred and fifty pounds and three tons, took seventeen days. Reports do not agree as to the exact number of crates; however, there were more than two hundred. The *Continental Gazette,* in a story about the departure of the crates, said that little was provided for the reception of the Statue, that the Pedestal should have been completed long ago, that a dozen of New

118

York's richest men could have provided for it. The newspaper praised *The World's* initiative and wrote:

These popular subscriptions show that there is a very real feeling on the subject of maintaining the national credit in the Bartholdi affair, and a determination to avert ridicule which a confession of disability to receive the magnificent French gift would bring down upon the United States.[13]

The *Isère* finally left Rouen on May 21 and arrived in New York on June 17. The ship was met outside New York harbor by the French North Atlantic Squadron, under Admiral Lacombe, and escorted into the port with flying colors. Commandant de Saune of the *Isère* presented the Statue of Liberty, still in crates, to General Stone. The parchment of transfer was signed by the President of the French Republic and by other officials, as well as by Auguste Bartholdi. On June 19 the *Isère* and her officers were given a rousing public reception including a parade through the city and a welcome at the New York City Hall. The arrival of the Statue of Liberty in New York is now commemorated every year by a ceremony near the base of the Statue of Liberty, organized by *L' Union Alsacienne* of New York with the cooperation of the other French societies of the city. It usually takes place on the Saturday nearest to June 17.

The unloading of the crates, which were placed near the Pedestal still under construction, began on June 22. Of course great interest was aroused by the arrival of Liberty at her future home. While the Statue was on its way to the United States *Harper's Weekly* published an article about the Pedestal, giving some precisions and measurements. The article said that this construction was erected inside the stone walls of the fort on Bedloe's Island and was worthy of the great figure which would stand on it, that its ornamentation prevented it from looking like a mere pyramid of stone, that it was built so as to direct all the attention to the Statue which would rest upon it. The paper also said that the foundation of the Pedestal was 91 feet square at the base and 66 feet, 7 inches square at the top, the Pedestal itself being 62 feet square at its base. It made its pyramidal ascent not like a continuous wall, but in a series of layers of stone. The Pedestal, *Harper's Weekly* continued, was resting upon a foundation which was 65 feet, 10 inches deep, the solidity of this

119

foundation being broken only by wide passageways through it at a level with the ground, and a circular vertical shaft in the middle which would be used for stairways and an elevator.[14] The public was also made familiar with other measurements of the future monument as they were given to the press by General Stone, chief engineer, namely 89 feet for the Pedestal; 151 feet, 1 inch for the height of the Statue's torch above the Pedestal; and 305 feet, 11 inches for the height of the torch above mean low water level.[15] More measurements were given now and again as the Statue was rising in the harbor and when it was completed. But as things stood in June 1885 there was still a great deal to do, and at that date *The World's* subscription campaign had not raised the full amount needed to complete the Pedestal.

The presence of the dismantled Statue in New York was naturally an incentive for *The World* to intensify its efforts. Thus, on the morning of June 19, when the men from the *Isère* got their official welcome, the newspaper announced that the subscription fund had reached $74,183.46. The $75,000 mark was passed that same day. Then, in an attempt to capitalize on the *Isère's* arrival in order to get the last quarter of the $100,000 as rapidly as possible, *The World* tried to follow a suggestion made by a Boston man shortly before the arrival of the French ship — to start a list of 100 names of persons willing to give $250 each. A total of 41 names were secured, but only 37 people gave their $250, although they were not required to do so since the 100 names had not been obtained. This, however, provided the handsome little sum of $6,750, and the list was discontinued as it was felt that it would be better to continue raising money from a general subscription.

The World continued its appeals and its publishing of long lists of names with amounts, great and small, as well as letters and cartoons. Although the paper continued to criticize the rich and scold the laggards the most critical phase of the campaign was over and there was no doubt that the goal would be reached shortly. When the $100,000 was about to be realized many people sent in very small amounts in the hope of being the last to make up the final sum. After Grant's funeral in August 1885 a group of ten people decided to walk home and sent their 50 cents in carfare to *The World*. They were not to be the last — a little more was needed to reach the goal! Sizable sums were still being received as was indicated by one of the letters sent in on the very eve of the great day.

Enclosed we take pleasure in handing you our check for $25 for the handsome Rochester lamp lately seen in our window for sale to assist in completing your great undertaking for the Bartholdi Pedestal.

With respect
Charles S. Upton, Manager[16]

Finally on August 11, 1885 *The World* proudly displayed this headline:

ONE HUNDRED THOUSAND DOLLARS
TRIUMPHANT COMPLETION OF THE
WORLD'S FUND FOR THE LIBERTY PEDESTAL

The gross total was actually $102,006.39, contributed by more than 120,000 people. *The World* sang its triumph in a six-stanza poem, without the author's name, starting like this:

Ah, Madame Liberty, God bless you!
Since all the cash is there at hand,
No longer need it now distress you
The question of a place to stand.

And the last stanza read:

Soon you in your allotted station,
Firm in your tower, strong and tall,
Will give this truth a new illustration,
THE PEOPLE ARE THE ALL IN ALL.

The last line of the poem was underlined.

An article explained that the success of this second campaign was due to a large extent to the much greater circulation of the newspaper. In May 1885 the circulation had passed the 150,000 mark, about seven times more than at the time of the first campaign. Moreover, in the meantime, as has already been pointed out, the newspaper had led the drive to elect Grover Cleveland to the presidency of the United States. The article added that the money had been raised in a relatively short time and gave as an example the Bunker Hill Monument Fund which had reached $150,000, but that it had taken eighteen years (1823-1842). It added that the $250,000 collected for General Grant had been given by a few wealthy men. Joseph Pulitzer and *The World* had reasons to be proud of their success. Congratulations poured in from all sides, some of which the New York newspaper was pleased to print. The *Hamilton Times* in Ontario, Canada, wrote: *"The World's* indomitable perseverance has saved our neighbors from a disgraceful humiliation." The *Buena Vista Democrat* in Colorado proclaimed:

One of the most sublime acts of the nineteenth century is the presentation of the priceless gift of the Bartholdi Statue of Liberty by the Republic of France to the Republic of the United States, as well as the unselfish and elevated act of the New York *WORLD* . . . and when completed will constitute an undying monument of the noble principles that govern this incomparable journal.[17]

The success of *The World's* campaign is commemorated by two mementos — one in Colmar, and the other in New York. In Colmar there is the large silver globe in Bartholdi's old home which was mentioned in the prologue. In New York there is the large stained-glass window with Liberty Enlightening the World which used to be in *The World's* Building on Park Row and is now in the Graduate School of Journalism of Columbia University, which Pulitzer's money helped to found. Few people who see the globe in Colmar or the stained-glass window in New York realize all the strenuous efforts on the part of Joseph Pulitzer and *The World's* staff which went into the twenty-one weeks of the campaign to raise the money necessary to complete the Pedestal of the Statue of Liberty.

The completion of the Pedestal took another eight months after the $100,000 was obtained, and Bartholdi decided to take another trip to the United States, his third, in order to confer with Chief Engineer Stone about the mounting of the Statue of Liberty. It will be remembered that the sculptor's first trip in 1871 to investigate the feasibility of his project had been *incognito* as far as the general public was concerned. The second one in 1876-77 had brought his name into the limelight. He had come as a member of the French delegation to the Centennial Exhibition in Philadelphia; his Lafayette statue had been unveiled in New York City; there were plans to erect the Statue of Liberty; and the Statue's arm was exhibited in Philadelphia. In 1885, after all the publicity which surrounded the fund-raising campaign for the Pedestal and with the Statue of Liberty in crates on Bedloe's Island, Bartholdi's arrival in New York on November 4, 1885 was to be quite an event. The time of his arrival was announced in the newspapers, and naturally the press was on hand in full force to interview the sculptor. Bartholdi's arrival had been preceded by considerable correspondence between the *Union Franco-Américaine* and the American Committee on the Statue of Liberty, and it had been deemed best for Bartholdi not to wait for Liberty's unveiling to come to America, but to arrive before the Statue was set up.

Auguste Bartholdi was accompanied by his wife. He wrote to his mother from the transatlantic steamer *Amérique,* a plan of which is among his papers, that the trip had been very good, except for the first few days when Jeanne was not feeling well. He added with his usual sense of humor that there was a gentleman aboard who said that he was traveling in order to be able to vomit, and that this had been prescribed by his doctor.[18] Bartholdi was very anxious to see how near completion the Pedestal was, and the artist's slim form was noticed on the deck of the steamer by tug watchers early in the morning as the ship was entering the narrows. A newspaper reporter, who had come to interview him, wrote that Bartholdi had hoped that the Pedestal would be further advanced and that it would be possible to mount the Statue before spring. He also wrote that Bartholdi had with him a model of the Lafayette monument which he would like to erect in the Nation's capital, adding that the sculptor had said that he was not going there to influence the committee, but to see his friends in Washington.[19] It has already been mentioned that he was to be disappointed about this project concerning which more will be said in due course. The sculptor was the first to come ashore. Many friends were awaiting him.

A press reporter described him in this manner:

A plain, modest, unpretentious man, dressed like a mechanic. He is of medium height, and has bold and rugged features. His head is rather large and his eyes are black. He was born in Alsace, and like all the stepchildren of France is devoted to her.[20]

Another reporter wrote that Bartholdi spoke English perfectly — a flattering statement with which Bartholdi would have been too modest to agree. Then came the usual type of tactless remarks that reporters in all English-speaking countries, today as well as yesterday, cannot help making when describing reunions of other people: "Being mostly Frenchmen, the embrace peculiar to that people was received and returned with such ardor that some minutes were occupied in that ceremony."[21]

No sooner was Bartholdi's name mentioned than the order was given to pass all his luggage without inspection. The artist said that he was hoping to return to France on November 25, because of business in Paris and the failing health of his mother. He gave his business address as 33 Mercer Street, which was at that time that of the American Committee on the Statue of Liberty, and asked that newspapers refrain from publishing his residence address. He did stay at the Hotel Hamilton at Fifth Avenue and 42nd Street, and the owner of this establishment, Mr. Jordan, later sent a photograph given to him by Bartholdi to the *Hotel Register* for publication. Bartholdi was asked by a reporter whether it was true that the French were impatient at the slowness of the contributions to the Pedestal Fund. To this the artist very diplomatically replied:

On the contrary, we have been very much pleased to see the money coming in so rapidly of late. The sum needed was a large one, and no one could expect that it would be subscribed in a day. I think America has done very well.[22]

While quite a bit of information is available on Bartholdi's social life during his third stay in the United States, the author has come across very little concerning the business side of the trip. It is assumed that the sculptor made one or more trips to Bedloe's Island to look at the state of the Pedestal and at the crates containing the disassembled Statue, that he had conferences with Chief Engineer Stone, who was to erect the Statue, and with the American Committee on the Statue of Liberty, particularly with Evarts and Butler. Little has come to light about Madame Bartholdi's activities, but it is certain that she did not accompany her husband all the time, not even to all the receptions, such functions in those days being often strictly men's affairs.

A great many invitations awaited Bartholdi on his arrival in America. Telegrams and letters have been preserved among his papers or those of his mother, which give some idea of the way the sculptor, who was in his early fifties, was lionized in 1885. A "Bartholdi Club" had been founded "to more prominently bring forward the name of a patriotic gentleman, lofty in his ideas, grand in his works, and friendly and loving to all Americans." There were twenty-five members in the club. The first annual public reception was to be held on November 23 at the Lyric Hall at 6th Avenue and 42nd Street. This club no longer exists and, as far as this author knows, there is not much left in New York City to "bring forward" Bartholdi's name. There is a decrepit Bartholdi Building, although the name is not indicated by any sign, at 23rd Street and Broadway. This was at one time the Hotel Bartholdi, an establishment of renown and a mecca for sportsmen from Madison Square Garden, which used to be nearby. Bartholdi's Inn near Times Square, a favorite meeting place for artists, has disappeared altogether. There is a Bartholdi street in The Bronx, one of the boroughs of New York City.

An inquiry made by this author a few years ago as to the reason why there were no plaques indicating that the Lafayette in Union Square and the Lafayette and Washington Monument near Morningside Park, on the edge of Harlem, were works by the creator of the Statue of Liberty brought a reply which is better forgotten than printed in these pages. The Bartholdi Club, the Bartholdi Hotel and Bartholdi's Inn have been the victims of a changing New York. As far as the two monuments just mentioned are concerned they are no longer in choice locations. It was mentioned that a plaque was placed only recently on "The Birthplace of the Statue of Liberty" in Paris. The French residents of New York are familiar with the Lafayette statue, and every year they hold a commemorative ceremony there. Maybe there is a plaque now.

Naturally, the Bartholdi Club expected the artist to be present at their first meeting. Moreover the members were to march in the parade on the day of Liberty's unveiling. A dinner was to be held at the Lotos Club in Bartholdi's honor on November 14 "to enable the members of the club to express their appreciation of his distinguished work in perpetuating the friendly and fraternal relations between the countries of Lafayette and Washington."[23] Bartholdi's invitation was signed by Th.W. Knox, secretary. Bartholdi penciled his reply accepting the invitation on the card, saying that he had had the surprise of receiving a telegram from the club shortly after leaving Le Havre. Pulitzer also wanted the pleasure of the company of the Bartholdis at dinner at 7 PM on November 18. Bartholdi preserved the invitation which was written in French. Pulitzer's address was given as 616 Fifth Avenue, New York. The executive committee of the American Committee on the Statue of Liberty had planned a dinner in Bartholdi's honor at the Union League Club on November 21. In connection with this invitation there is a letter addressed to Richard Butler by Charles Butler of 78 Park Avenue in which this author found the following passage of interest:

As Lafayette died in the same year in which Bartholdi, your distinguished guest, was born, it would seem as if Providence had made provision to preserve and perpetuate in some visible form the spirit which animated the heart of Lafayette, and moved him to leave home and country and give himself to the course of liberty in this then new land.[24]

Faced by so many invitations Bartholdi requested a couple of days of rest before getting involved in all the merry-go-round of public appearances. He wrote to his mother that he went from one reception to the other, that he had dinner with former United States President Arthur and was meeting people who were interesting "by the millions they represented," but that there was no news about his Lafayette project for Washington, D.C.[25] Apparently the rich people who had stayed in hiding during *The World's* campaign were now jumping on the bandwagon and trying to make up for their earlier lack of support. It is probable that Bartholdi visualized the many commissions for busts or statues that he might get from such wealthy people. These hopes, however, were not to materialize.

Bartholdi gave a farewell dinner on Sunday, November 22, at the Richelieu. The menu has been preserved among Bartholdi's papers. He left with his wife, as scheduled, on November 25 aboard the *Normandie*. He found aboard a telegram from A. Brunel, president of the Liberty Guards of Hudson County, New Jersey, thanking him for accepting the honorary presidency of the society whose members said Brunel:

126

wish you a speedy and joyful journey and hope that you may soon return to the country which owes you the Statue of Liberty which cements the union of two republics and immortalizes your name.

with you a useful and joyful journey, and hope that you may again return to the country which gives you the statue of Liberty which augments the union of two republics and immortalizes your name.

CHAPTER EIGHT

The Erection of the Statue of Liberty in New York Harbor and the Preparations for the Unveiling

Because of the unavoidable delays during the winter, the Pedestal was not completed until the spring of 1886. A ceremony was held on April 22 attended by a number of officials and presided over by Chief Engineer Stone. A block of granite weighing two tons was suspended near a six-foot opening. When Stone announced that he wanted to set the last stone of the Pedestal in silver, a shower of dimes, quarters, halves, and dollars fell into the mortar and the block was lowered in place. In a speech which he made on this occasion Stone claimed that the Pedestal had been raised without a single man having been either killed or injured.

Soon after this ceremony the mounting of the Statue of Liberty started and went on for several months, the last piece being placed only shortly before the unveiling on October 28, 1886. This piece was the sole of the right foot, which had been left open in order to let workers go in and out of the Statue. The size of the sole was approximately nine feet long by four feet wide. The press kept the public informed about the progress of the work on Bedloe's Island, publishing now and again pictures of the Statue as it gradually rose above the Pedestal. Some of these pictures were amusing, such as a man sitting on Liberty's thumb or another standing near a lock of her hair.[1]

The first thing to be done in mounting the Statue was naturally to anchor properly the massive framework designed by Gustave Eiffel. The latter had given instructions in this respect which were checked over on the spot by Stone and Bartholdi on the occasion of the latter's third visit to the United States. As far as this author knows Eiffel did not come to Bedloe's Island to supervise the mounting of the Statue. The framework was designed in order to enable Liberty to withstand the strongest gales of the bay, and with some repairs it has held firm to this day.

When Liberty's first two copper plates — the first called Bartholdi, and the second Pulitzer — were riveted onto the framework there was another ceremony which took place on July 12, 1886. It is strange that the organizers of this ceremony did not wait for another two days to make it correspond with the French National Day, July 14. All the pieces making up the Statue had been carefully numbered before being put into the crates. However, some of the huge sections that had been crated for so long and shaken in transportation had been somewhat flattened out of their original shapes, and it took some time to reshape them. In some cases there had been a mix-up in labeling or some of the numbers had come off the pieces. The problem got more and more complicated as the Statue grew in height, so that it was sometimes necessary to hoist successively two or three pieces until the right one was found. When Liberty was mounted in Paris, the structure was surrounded by scaffoldings on which the men were working. In New York, however, probably on account of the Pedestal, another method was used. Men were working from seats and planks attached by cables to the framework of the Statue or to the Statue itself. From a distance they looked like insects crawling on a gown.

Not satisfied to rest on its laurels after the completion of the campaign to raise the $100,000 *The World* undertook by various means to raise some more money to help with the setting up of Liberty on her Pedestal. Shortly after the completion of the latter a big dance was given in Madison Square Garden, with the band of the 22nd Regiment furnishing the music. A newspaper wrote an article about it under the title of "Soldiers aiding Liberty." This paper estimated that the last $15,000 needed by *The World* to finish setting Liberty on her Pedestal was well on its way as a result of this entertainment. It was figured that the proceeds would net the Bartholdi Fund" more than two thirds of the amount needed.[2] It was fortunate that the money was no longer coming in the form of pennies and dimes.

This time Congress also rose to the occasion and appropriated $56,500 for various expenses, including the cost of unveiling Liberty. However, this was not as much as had been requested.[3] Information which reached a French newspaper sounded as if this bill also had not passed. An American newspaper man had commented that the bill had been amended by the Senate in such a way that no money could be spent on wine and liquor. The House had let the bill stand, and the President had signed it. "A rather unusual effort," the writer of the article pointed out, "to ruin the digestions and tempers of a few innocent French officials, by making them drink nothing but Croton water for a week."[4] (Croton was, and still is, a reservoir from which water used in New York came.) Matters were arranged later on, and champagne was served at the official banquet at Delmonico's.

A reporter from the *New York Tribune* took a trip to Bedloe's Island on a small steamer which made the trip every hour on Sundays about one month before the unveiling of the Statue of Liberty. The figure looked to him half Grecian, half French. Many pieces were still lying on the ground, such as the crown which looked like a mere ring with spikes. Inside the Statue there was only a winding wooden staircase and the visitor could hear broken bolts and rivets falling down the shaft where the elevator now runs. At that time the view from Bedloe's Island was very different from what it is today. The reporter said:

The Battery, looking fresh and pretty in the distance, sets off strikingly the deep red of the Produce Exchange Building, whose tall square tower is easily the central point on the picture. The Washington Building, the yellowish Cotton Exchange, the spire of Trinity, the tower of the Western Union and the Tribune Building strike the eye at a glance, and beyond, just on the limit of vision, is the white landmark of Grace Church spire.[5]

At first it was hoped that there could be a September unveiling, but finally the date of October 28 was selected and kept. Preparations, however, started long before that date, and there was an exchange of letters between Bartholdi and Butler concerning the

130

membership of the French delegation. The sculptor was worried because the official invitation from the United States Government was delayed. Also his mother's health made him fear that he would not be able to attend the unveiling of "my daughter."

The main features of the October 28 celebration were to be a land parade through the streets of the city, a naval parade on the Hudson River and in the harbor, and an unveiling ceremony at Bedloe's Island. There was also to be an official banquet at night. President Grover Cleveland was to attend the first three events. It was a strange coincidence that it happened to be the same Cleveland who, as governor of New York State, had vetoed in 1884 as unconstitutional a bill passed by the State legislature appropriating $50,000 for work on the Pedestal.[6] This author has found the mass of information in the newspapers — both in the United States and abroad — concerning the preparations for Liberty's unveiling and the unveiling itself sometimes contradictory. And it is no wonder since there must have been great confusion at times. The parade in the rain through the streets of Manhattan was disrupted at one time by a fire engine with accompanying vehicles racing in the opposite direction from the parade. During the unveiling ceremony on the island, a signal was mistaken and there was a pandemonium of ships' sirens and whistles in the fog of the harbor which seriously disturbed the proceedings at the foot of the Statue of Liberty. Finally, the ceremony was followed by a shameful and hectic rush for the boats which the police on duty were unable to control.

One may say that the whole unveiling affair started on Sunday night, October 24, when the steamship *La Bretagne* bringing the French delegation to the United States arrived at the New York quarantine station. Aboard were Ferdinand de Lesseps, accompanied by his young daughter Tototte who had been sick during the whole voyage, and Auguste Bartholdi and his wife. It is not clear whether the other passengers were official guests, newspaper correspondents or persons who had come on their own. There had been quite a bit of correspondence between Paris and New York about this with many changes concerning those who were supposed to come and those who actually did come. Of this the press was not aware. Also the spelling of names varied in the reports. There were an admiral and a general who came as delegates of the French Senate, and the French Chamber of Deputies also sent two of its members. A reporter from *The World* went out in a boat to *La Bretagne* to interview Bartholdi. Although the sea was so rough that he could not attempt to board the ship, he was able to send a note to Bartholdi with Pulitzer's compliments and asking what the voyage had been like. Copies of *The World* were pulled aboard with the note. Bartholdi replied that the voyage had been excellent, that he was pleased to come to America, and that he took pride in "the old friendship which has always united the two nations with one single thought 'Liberty'." The sculptor, wearing a close-fitting sea cap, came on deck to greet *The World's* reporter. In the course of the conversation that took place, Bartholdi said that he had been trying to see the Statue's light. . . Alas, "Liberty Enlightening the World" was not to shine for quite a while. Plans had called for the main light in the torch to have 30,000 candle power, but the first light in the torch was hardly visible from a distance and some compared it to a glowworm. Lesseps also came on deck, and the sculptor said to the eighty-one-year-old builder of the Suez Canal: "Mr. de Lesseps, you would not have been enjoying this breeze from the American shore now if it had not been for *The World*. Is it not so?" As the boat with the reporter aboard was leaving the French people on *La Bretagne* shouted: "*Vive le Monde!*" (Long live *The World*).[7]

The following day, October 25, *La Bretagne* steamed into the harbor and was met by the yacht *Tillie*, aboard which was the American welcoming committee, which included Joseph Pulitzer, who had been the last to catch the boat and had climbed aboard panting and puffing. While the *Tillie* and the ocean steamer were still apart, Madame Bartholdi noticed some of her friends aboard the yacht and greeted them from a distance. She wore a well-fitting dress of blue serge and a felt hat with green and black feathers, and carried a bunch of roses with a tricolor ribbon. The whole French delegation was taken aboard the *Tillie*, and as the yacht sailed towards Bedloe's Island, the sun shone on the Statue of Liberty which was "glistening like gold." When the yacht neared the island Madame Bartholdi, whose eyes filled with tears, pressed the hand of Mrs. Glaenzer, Evarts' daughter, and exclaimed: "How beautiful!"

During the visit at Bedloe's Island newspaper reporters were all around — representing the *New York Tribune, The New York*

Herald, and naturally *The World* — anxious to write down the remarks which they heard from members of the French delegation. They were particularly keen to catch Bartholdi's first impressions. "I am much pleased," he said to a *Herald* reporter after he had stood in silence for a while. "It is a grand sight. I was worried about some of the lines. It is a success."[8] When the sculptor was at the Pedestal he tapped on one of its corners and remarked: "I have always liked this Egyptian style. I hope that this base will last as long as the pyramids along the Nile."[9] At another time, and this remark was picked up by the ever viligant *World* reporter, Bartholdi said: "The dream of my life is accomplished; I see the symbol of unity and friendship between two nations — two great republics.[10] Then, talking to Lesseps he observed: "It is a consolation to know that this statue will exist thousands of years from now, long after our names shall have been forgotten." Much of what the artist said, however, must have been lost as far as American reporters were concerned, as one of them wrote that while Bartholdi spoke English slowly he spoke it well, but "his French is an animated torrent to the inexperienced listener."

Ferdinand de Lesseps, who had accomplished great things at Suez and was hoping to accomplish greater things yet at Panama, could not help expressing his admiration, and exclaimed: "It has surpassed my expectations. I was prepared for a great work of art, but this is sublime. It is simply faultless."[11] Upon arrival at the island Lesseps and other members of the French delegation had removed their hats at the sight of Bartholdi's work. Praise and flattery were pouring in from all sides. Mr. Pelletier, a member of the French delegation, went to the extent of saying: "Indeed, Liberty Island was created for Bartholdi's Statue, not the Statue for the island!" As far as the island was concerned, Bartholdi said that he would have preferred that the ground slope gradually from the water to the Pedestal and that the walls of the fort not be as visible as they were, and still are. The visit at Bedloe's Island was an unforgettable experience for many. Young Tototte had a grand time running around in and near the Statue. She got a small piece of granite from the Pedestal and treasured it as "Liberty's Rock."[12]

Newspapers were now vying with each other in publishing articles, more or less correct, about the story of the Statue of Liberty and preparations for the coming unveiling. Criticisms, however, were still to be found here and there. A newspaper claimed that Launt Thompson, a sculptor, had said that Liberty stood on the wrong leg and that Bartholdi had violated the simplest rule of science and art in the pose of his colossal woman. Other sculptors were also critical, but did not want to be quoted. One of the critics said that the drapery had been handled so badly that from a distance the Statue gave no conception of the human form, that from the Battery the Statue looked like a bag of potatoes with a stick projecting from it, and that Liberty belonged more to architecture than to sculpture. To top all this, one of the most distinguished sculptors in America was quoted as having stated that: "From an artistic standpoint, the Pedestal is vastly superior to the Statue."[13] After the dedication of the Statue of Liberty it appears that some artists changed their minds or at least did not want to look like troublemakers amidst the general enthusiasm. The day after the unveiling *The World* published an article on the Statue of Liberty "as a work of Art" with some favorable comments by artists. One of them, Eastman Johnson, said that he had no sympathy with critics of the Statue and of the motives of Bartholdi and France. "As a colossal work it is magnificent and thoroughly successful," he declared.[14] Even Launt Thompson was reported to have praised the way Bartholdi had been able to sustain such a large mass, although he still maintained that it should be looked at architecturally rather than artistically.[15]

Generally speaking artists are critical of one another's work, and Auguste Bartholdi was no exception. It has been mentioned that he found fault with the dome of the Capitol in Washington when he went there in 1871 and also with the Washington Monument, which at that time was under construction. This monument is nothing but a giant obelisk, a form of architecture going back to Ancient Egypt, whose art the sculptor liked so much. Later, when he was not commissioned to make a Lafayette Monument in Washington, he wrote a letter criticizing its design.[16] Had Bartholdi been able to erect his own Lafayette, a model of which is in Colmar, the chances are that some people would have found fault with it, since art is to a large extent a matter of taste which varies with the people and with the times.

While a number of artists continued to remain cold or even hostile to the Statue of Liberty, poets, unconcerned with rules of sculpture or science and not envious of a foreign colleague, sang Liberty far and wide, expressing in verse what they felt in their hearts. Such feelings, already expressed by Emma Lazarus and others during the fund-raising campaign for the Pedestal, were to blossom in a number of poems which were published around the time of the Statue's unveiling.

Here are stanzas from a few of these poems:

Oh ye, whose broken spars
Tell of the storms ye met,
Enter! there are no bars
Across your pathway set.
Enter at Freedom's porch,
For you I lift my torch,
For you my coronet
Is rayed with stars.

Edmund C. Stedman (5th stanza) [17]

Rise, stately Symbol! holding forth
Thy light and hope to all who sit
In chains and darkness; Belt the earth
With watch fires from thy torch uplit.

John Greenleaf Whittier (4th stanza) [18]

And hither, ye weary ones and breathless,
    searching the seas for a kindly shore,
I am Liberty! patient, deathless, — set by Love
    at the Nation's door!
Liberty Enlightening the World.

John Boyle O'Reilly (closing lines of a long poem) [19]

At the same time as it published O'Reilly's poem *The World* gave the story of its author, an Irish Fenian who had been exiled by the British to Australia and had made a dramatic escape to the United States. It has been mentioned in connection with the poem of Emma Lazarus that the longest poem on Liberty this author came across was by C. P. Schermerhorn. Here is the first of its twenty-one stanzas.

On freedom's soil doth stand,
At the gateway of the sea,
On pedestal tall and grand,
A Goddess of Liberty.[20]

Such poems expressed what people were to feel more and more about the symbolism of the Statue of Liberty as time passed on. However, the gift was to cement Franco-American friendship, and there were also poems composed with this in mind. Bartholdi also got his laurels from the poets, both in France and in America, as in this last stanza of a poem by Noah Davis, which appeared on the day of the unveiling in *The Independent,* a New York paper:

And thou Bartholdi! genius-crowned son of France and Art
Confrere right worthy of immortals! Now
Columbia's grateful laurels wreathe thy brow,
For thine hath been the patriot sculptor's nobler part,
To weld in bronze a century's love of Peoples, heart to heart.[21]

Bartholdi and the French delegation stayed at Hoffman House, the exclusive hotel on Broadway, between 24th and 25th Streets. A series of receptions and dinners were planned in honor of Bartholdi and the French delegation which were to be climaxed with the unveiling ceremony. However, these celebrations did not end with the unveiling of the Statue and would have lasted for quite a while had not obligations at home cut short the stay of the sculptor and most of the delegates.

The delegates had been offered lunch aboard the yacht *Tillie,* but the first official banquet was at Hoffman House on the evening of October 25. On the following day they were officially received by the American Committee on the Statue of Liberty at the Academy of Music. There were speeches, of course, and singing in English and in French. Evarts spoke in the name of the American Committee, and Eugene Spuller, a journalist and a politician, who had distinguished himself in the Franco-Prussian War, replied in the name of the *Union Franco-Américaine,* saying: "We are proud that the Statue was made by a Frenchman; we are still more proud that it was made by an Alsatian." Elderly Ferdinand de Lesseps could not help standing up and embracing Spuller on the platform. At this the whole audience rose and cheered.[22] An English-speaking reporter, however, who was present, contemptuously referred to this as "Gallic fervor," although there were quite a number of non-French people who shared in this enthusiasm.

On October 27, in a ceremony which took place at 1 PM at City Hall, Bartholdi was officially received by Mayor Grace of New York and presented with the Freedom of the City. The enframed diploma is now hanging in one of the rooms of the *Musée Bartholdi* in Colmar. A reproduction of it was published in the local newspapers on the occasion of the visit in Colmar of A. Houghton, Ambassador of the United States to France, in August 1959. Not much time was given to the artist to get over the excitement of this ceremony. The same afternoon, at 2:15 PM, he was taken to the Produce Exchange where a glee club sang *The Marseillaise*. Bartholdi was embarrassed when he was asked to make a speech, because of the language problem, and because he felt that he did not know a great deal about trade.

As the French delegation was taken through New York City, reporters were always on hand making notes of their impressions. For instance, they did not care for the elevated trains and preferred the London Underground. At the same time the public was fed news of all sorts, sometimes contradictory, about the preparations for the unveiling day. Such information was given by the newspapers as — there would be no women at the ceremony on Bedloe's Island; no tickets had been issued to ladies and "those who might try to slip through are warned that crush will be great";[23] the ladies of the French delegation were expected to watch the proceedings from the deck of a warship. As it turned out some women attended the ceremony at the Statue, including Madame Bartholdi and Tototte de Lesseps, but it was true that the crush was great. The New York State Woman Suffrage Association announced that they had hired a boat to cruise near the Statue of Liberty during the ceremony and that speeches would be made on the boat praising Liberty embodied as a woman and raising the hope of all women.[24] Things have changed a great deal since 1886. American women have the right to vote, and they are now the ones who are running the anniversary ceremony at the Statue of Liberty each year on October 28. It has been previously pointed out that this ceremony is organized by the Ladies Auxiliary to Veterans of Foreign Wars of the United States. Men are allowed to come to the Statue on that day; some are even invited to make speeches and Bartholdi's name is usually mentioned in one of them, but it is largely a women's day, and it is quite a sight to see them marching with their unfurled flags.

The press reported that only 3,500 tickets had been issued by the American Committee on the Statue of Liberty to guests invited to attend the ceremony on the island and that only people in the grand stand would be able to hear speeches. A police force of two hundred and fifty men was to keep order before and during the ceremony. This number proved inadequate. It was reported that the New York police had been warned by other cities that crooks were leaving for New York. Some arrests had already been made, giving some people free board and room during their brief stay in the city. Over one hundred detectives were assigned to mingle with the crowds, and it was hoped that people with watches and other valuables would be relatively safe.

The Union League Club of New York granted membership privileges to all the French delegates during their stay in the city, and held an elaborate reception on the eve of the unveiling. The reception committee included John Pierpont Morgan, Theodore Roosevelt, William Evarts, Elihu Root, and other prominent people. Drexel had lent for the occasion the Moran painting of Liberty which has already been mentioned. Chauncey M. Depew, president of the club, was one of the persons who was scheduled to speak at Bedloe's Island the next day. An elaborate centerpiece on the serving table represented the Statue of Liberty, George Washington and Lafayette. Other items of Franco-American interest such as the frigate *La Minerve* and the Column of the Bastille were represented in confectionery. The menu was printed in French. This reception was attended by a number of the officers from the French warships that had sailed into the harbor to join the naval parade. Among the rumors which had circulated before the unveiling was one that the French warships would not be able to arrive in time for the ceremony.

One of the debated questions was whether October 28 would be a holiday. The *New York Tribune* published a letter from the New York Stock Exchange stating that they could only close down on Sundays and legal bank holidays on account of their ramifications all over the country. The Board of Education hesitated about closing schools because of turning thousands of pupils loose into the streets of the City of New York.

According to the newspapers more and more organizations wanted to join the parade; even some "secret" societies like the Knights of Pythias had applied for spaces. The list of prospective participants in the parade grew longer and longer as the days went by. There were to be also out-of-town groups coming from as far away as Philadelphia, which was going to send a delegation of policemen, and Baltimore, from where firemen were to come. Theaters had agreed to open their doors only at 8:30 or 9 PM in order to let their patrons view the fireworks which were planned for the night of the 28th. In this connection, files of one hundred soldiers each were to be arranged in such a way that the colored lights which each group would burn would alternately compose the French and American flags.

The beflagging of the city along the way of the parade started very early. "I am selling so many French flags that I am forgetting my English," a Fulton Street flag dealer was reported to have said.[25] The Hotel Bartholdi located close to the place where the presidential reviewing stand was to be at Madison Square Park, was decorated with rows of flags on both its facades. In Park Row a triumphal arch made of evergreens, sixty feet tall in the center, had been erected between *The World's* Building and the Post Office. Announcements were made that the railroad companies would run special excursion trains into the city on the 28th. Mayor Grace had issued a proclamation recommending storekeepers to close shop during the parade and those stores along the streets of the parade to put out flags. New York City public offices were to be closed.

The route of the parade was to be four miles long, starting at 57th Street, going down Fifth Avenue, and, in places where the paving did not permit, down Madison Avenue, then down Broadway, and ending at the Battery. President Grover Cleveland was to come from Washington with some of the members of his cabinet to review the parade, together with Bartholdi, Lesseps, and the other officials, when it reached Madison Square Park. After the parade the President of the United States was expected to embark at the 23rd Street pier to take the trip to Bedloe's Island where his arrival was to be announced by a twenty-one-gun salute. However, many things did not quite work the way they had been planned as is to be expected when so many people are involved.

CHAPTER NINE

The Statue of Liberty is Unveiled Amidst Great Festivities on October 28, 1886

Finally the morning of Thursday, October 28, arrived. People in large numbers came to the city. The crowds reminded reporters of the year before on the occasion of former President Grant's funeral. It was estimated that about one million people attended the parades of that day. This was considerable because according to the census of 1880 New York's population was estimated at 1,911,000. Many families came in very early carrying wooden boxes to stand on; some came all the way from Brooklyn — across the river from Manhattan where the parade was to take place. Many came on horseback. Rain started falling about nine o'clock that morning, but people stayed in their places, hoisting umbrellas. Umbrella vendors made a thriving business on that day, while soda vendors hardly made any sales. Hundreds of people stood on top of piles of stones which had been taken out of Fifth Avenue, in preparation for repaving between 26th and 28th Streets. Some store owners put chairs on boxes to the indignation of the people whose view of the parade would be obstructed, "yet nobody interfered since it was not a money-making speculation."[1] In other cases, however, it was, and people who had been allowed to stand on boxes free were dispossessed when paying customers arrived. Seats on horse cars, parked nearby, were rented anywhere from 10 to 50 cents each. Below 33rd Street there were several buildings under repair. People succeeded in getting upon the scaffolding and sitting on the projecting rafters to watch the parade go by.

Before the parade, wagons went up and down the empty streets advertising products as long as the police did not interfere. On one of them came a man dressed up to represent Bartholdi who distributed leaflets. Commemorative medals were being sold with the Statue of Liberty on the one side and Bartholdi's likeness on the other. Pictures of Bartholdi were also peddled. Even pictures of the Brooklyn Bridge were sold at one cent a piece. Credulous Italians, who had recently immigrated to the United States, were made to believe that it was Bartholdi's work. Some of them probably believed that he was one of their countrymen. The sculptor's name, now nearly forgotten, was on everyone's lips, while references to "Bartholdi Day" were found as frequently in the press as those to "Liberty Day." Hundreds of carriages parked in the area of the Windsor Hotel on Fifth Avenue, between 46th and 47th Streets, were awaiting some of the distinguished participants in the parade, and in the meantime nearly one thousand impatient horses pawing and neighing made a great deal of noise.

It was estimated that twenty thousand people participated in the land parade. They were divided into ten divisions, usually composed of several different groups. The general organization of the parades and ceremonies was under the supervision of Major General J. M. Scholfield, who had started the preparations long before October 28. The first division organized in the area of 57th Street and marched down Fifth Avenue, reaching the presidential reviewing stand at Madison Square Park about 11 AM.

President Grover Cleveland, who had spent the night in the home of Secretary of the Navy Whitney, arrived shortly before the first division reached the stand. Introductions were made. Ferdinand de Lesseps was the first to be introduced to the President, then Auguste Bartholdi. President Cleveland greeted him with a smile and said: "You are the greatest man in America today!" "Through your courtesy," replied the Frenchman bowing before the Chief Executive.[2] Finding to their surprise that all the seats were wet on account of the rain, the President and the honored guests remained standing during the whole parade in a drizzling rain. Now and again, Lesseps, who was probably the oldest man in the stand, showed that he was uncomfortable by stamping the boards with his feet to aid circulation. The President kept smiling all the time. He was effusive in his returning of salutes when Italian or colored groups came by, and it was said that the election campaign of 1888 was already under way. Reporters from France were particularly impressed by a company of Negroes that marched along — some dark like ebony while others were nearly white.

General Stone, who had been in charge of the building of the Pedestal and of the erection of the Statue of Liberty, served as the Grand Marshal, and mounted on a black horse led the parade. When he arrived at the reviewing stand, he joined the President and the people who were already there. The first division of the parade was military. The French guests were thrilled when the band of the Seventh Regiment approached the stand, playing *The Marseillaise*. As a matter of fact, the French national anthem was to be one of the most frequently played airs during the parade. The playing by different bands not sufficiently apart produced discordant effects at times. The second division was partly military, partly civilian. It included the French-speaking societies of the city, which were led by the now non-existent *Société Colmarienne* in order to pay tribute to Colmar, Bartholdi's home town. Of course, *L' Union Alsacienne* of New York was there too, and there was also one group called *Mardi Gras* Association, which does not exist anymore. One of the largest French groups was the *Société Israélite*, made up of Jewish people of French origin, many of whom were from Alsace. This society is still active. There were also two companies of *Gardes Rochambeau*, dressed in period uniforms. In the same division were carriages with judges and governors. In the third and fourth divisions, except for the mayors of various cities, there were chiefly war veterans. One hundred carriages held members of the Aztec Society, formed by veteran officers of the War with Mexico. Three veterans of the War of 1812, the youngest of them eighty-seven years old, were supposed to take part in the parade. They waited at Military Hall for a couple of hours. When no one came to pick them up, they got angry and went away, saying that never again would they agree to take part in a parade because this was not the first time that they had been forgotten.

The fifth division, largely formed by the Grand Army of the Republic, had been assigned several streets for organization, because of the large number of participants. The sixth division was formed by veteran military organizations. The seventh had United States volunteers and a particularly lively group of college students, led by Columbia College. Every now and then could be heard the shouts: "Hurrah! H! H! C-O-L-U-M-B-I-A or C-C-N-Y, Hurrah!" This second yell came from students of City College, New York. After the name of the college invariably came B-A-R-T-H-O-L-D-I.[3] It is amusing to read in a French newspaper the English sounds of the letters spelled out for the benefit of the readers. Immediately behind the students came the Bartholdi Club, now about one year old and fifty members strong. The leader carried a banner with a miniature torch of the Statue of Liberty in bronze, which had been presented to the organization by Bartholdi himself.

The eighth division was formed by independent military organizations. Featured in this section of the parade was George Washington's carriage pulled by eight horses; on it was a flag which was associated with Abraham Lincoln, another famous President of the United States. The ninth division was formed by organizations from Brooklyn, and the tenth and last division by volunteer firemen and other organizations. Naturally fire engines — some very old ones — were also included. Towards the end of the parade there was a float with a floral representation of the Statue of Liberty, with the face made of wax.

Many people were walking along with the parade, massing themselves at several successive places to see it come by. Newspapermen were stationed at a number of places, and they have left us vivid accounts of the parade, particularly of what happened around the reviewing stand where President Cleveland, Bartholdi, and the other officials were standing and shivering, and also in the neighborhood of *The World* Building further downtown.

An interesting incident occurred when the Grand Army of the Republic came by the President's reviewing stand. Three little girls left the ranks, walked toward the stand, and presented baskets full of flowers artistically arranged. They said: "For Mr. Bartholdi." The President replied: "Thank you." Then one of them opened up a silken banner. When an assistant of the President took it, she

143

cried nervously: "That's for Mr. Bartholdi," as if she was afraid that the President might get it. On the one side of the banner was a French flag, and on the other side a United States flag. There was also an inscription which read:

To M. Bartholdi
In Memory of Liberty-Loving France
New York, 1886
Presented by May Fest.[4]

No wonder the little girl was anxious that no one else but Bartholdi should get it! The President remembered the three little girls who had presented him with flowers the preceding year at the time of Grant's funeral. The last of the ten divisions went past the reviewing stand shortly after one o'clock, and the President left. He still had to attend a naval parade and a ceremony on Bedloe's Island.

At *The World's* arch on Park Row a large number of people was waiting, singing songs, and occasionally shouting cheers for *The World*, Bartholdi, and Liberty. When the Sixty-Ninth Regiment arrived, it stopped before the arch and presented arms in recognition for the great efforts of the newspaper in the fund-raising campaign for the Pedestal. When the First and Second Batteries arrived near the arch, a reporter of *The World* overheard the following conversation between two little boys perched on the arch: "Say, Billy, does you think they's loaded?" "Don't know. Guess so," was the answer. "Well, I don't care if they are, Billy, they won't shoot at *The World* anyway, and we are safe."[5] When some popular regiment went by the people surged forward, pushing those who were in front into the street. Policemen using clubs had to push them back. A young man tried to push his way through the crowd, claiming he was a reporter for *The World*. He was stopped by a police line and was told that many had tried the same trick before. He was advised to think of something else: "That *World* racket is played out."[6] A visitor from the countryside was said to have believed that *The World* Building was the City Hall of New York because all the paraders saluted it as they passed. It was a great day indeed for *The World*, and well deserved too.

As the Baltimore firemen were passing under *The World's* arch, a woman's cry was heard in the crowd: "Oh, my watch!" Pointing to a man who was trying to sneak away, the woman yelled: "Yes, that's

144

the man!" The man was dragged to where the woman stood and the watch was found on him. Some people were going to call the police when a man came along and said: "I'll show you how one treats such fellows,"[7] and he kicked the thief who, after that, disappeared into the crowd. A newspaper reported that there had been thirty preventive arrests of professional thieves before the parade and that ten more had been picked up during the parade. Anyway, this one got away.

When the last group of paraders had passed under *The World's* arch, a little boy was heard to shout: "Say, I got a piece of the arch." He held out a branch of hemlock, and people rushed to the arch and tore off pieces of greenery as souvenirs. A business-minded lad climbed up the arch and sold branches at 5 cents a piece. The land parade ended at the Battery, at the lower end of Manhattan Island facing the Statue of Liberty. However, many groups had left the procession below Wall Street and disbanded in the side streets.

The next phase of the unveiling ceremonies was the naval parade. Plans called for the ships, three hundred in all of various descriptions, to leave the area around West 42nd Street, sail down the Hudson River, and form a crescent in the harbor below Bedloe's Island. They were to salute the Statue of Liberty with their guns, whistles, or sirens as soon as the flag covering Liberty's face was removed. This was to be a grand sight — reminiscent of Moran's painting of Liberty surrounded by many ships. As it turned out, however, October 28 was not a clear day. It had rained during the land parade. Then, fog prevented the naval parade from being the great show it might have been and even, as will be seen, interfered with the proceedings on Bedloe's Island. When one reads the accounts of the happenings on October 28, one wonders why such a day in the fall was selected for the unveiling. The erection of the Statue of Liberty had lasted for such a long time that it seems that it should not have made much difference if the unveiling had been postponed until the following spring. As a matter of fact, there was still work to be done on the Statue of Liberty shortly before the unveiling, which had been originally planned for September. There were still many unsightly things around on Bedloe's Island, although most of the trash had been moved to one part of the island. The weather also prevented the firework display planned for the night of the 28th.

While there may be some very beautiful days late in October, the weather in New York at this time of the year is rather unpredictable, and this is one of the reasons why the French-speaking societies of New York now have their ceremony at the Statue of Liberty in June, commemorating its arrival in 1885.

At a gun signal given at 12:45 PM the ships fell in line and started moving slowly and majestically down the Hudson River which floods had rendered muddy. On account of the fog, they looked from a distance like nautical ghosts gliding downstream. The most important warship in the parade was the *Tennessee,* flagship of the North Atlantic Squadron. There were also French warships and a large number of other boats. The steamship companies with piers along the Hudson had vied with one another to decorate their installations. The *Dispatch* that had picked up the President to take him to Bedloe's Island passed in front of the ships. The Chief Executive waved with his handkerchief to his friends on the *Tennessee.* His arrival at the island was accompanied by a twenty-one-gun salute from all the warships. The smoke from the guns mixed with the fog completely hid the Statue of Liberty for a while. The President reached Bedloe's Island, which was sometimes referred to in press accounts as "Liberty Island," about 3 PM. Landing was not an easy matter. The *Dispatch* was too large to come alongside the pier, so the President had to get into a launch that in turn discharged him on a float from which a ladder led to the pier. President Cleveland looked at the ladder for a moment, then, when help was offered him, he climbed up as rapidly as his weight would permit.

Between three and four thousand people were waiting for the President to arrive — they had started embarking at the Battery about 1 PM. There had been a scramble to get ashore, one of the New York City aldermen nearly falling into the water when trying to jump. There were American and French flags everywhere. The French flag which veiled Liberty's countenance looked like a handkerchief on her broad face. The speaker's platform was surmounted by a large banner, on which was inscribed in large letters: A BARTHOLDI and LIBERTY.

A band had been playing most of the time during the landing and seating of the President and other officials, which included the Secretary of State. The meeting was called to order by Major Gen-

146

eral Scholfield, the master of ceremonies. After the firing of a signal gun Reverend Richard S. Storrs, a minister from Brooklyn, gave the invocation which ended with the Lord's Prayer. Ferdinand de Lesseps, speaking in the name of the *Union Franco-Américaine,* of which he was the president, made a presentation address. Reverend Storrs' invocation had concluded under unfavorable conditions with ships' horns blowing in the fog out in the harbor. The noise increased during Lesseps' speech and he remarked humorously: "Steam was invented as a benefit, and its progress is wonderful, but at present it is an evil and retards the progress of my speech."[8] There were cheers in the audience. The speaker, who was often referred to in the press as "Le Grand Français," (the Great Frenchman) spoke in French, and was probably understood by only a small fraction of the listeners. As Lesseps, who was bare-headed, spoke Tototte stood behind her father. He said: "There are no disagreeable or sorrowful recollections between the two nations. They have but one rivalry — progress. We accept your inventions, as you accept ours, without envy."[9] The builder of the Suez Canal ended his speech with these words:

Soon, gentlemen, we will meet together again to celebrate another pacific conquest. "Au revoir" at Panama, where the 38-star flag of North America will come to float next to the banners of the independent countries of South America in order to form in the New World, for the good of mankind, the pacific and fruitful alliance of the Franco-Latin race with the Anglo-Saxon race.[10]

The poor man was far from imagining what was to happen to his Panama Canal project a few years later.

After the applause which followed Lesseps' speech, the people insisted on hearing a speech by Bartholdi, who had been introduced to the audience earlier in the proceedings. Getting impatient Major General Scholfield shouted: "Mr. Bartholdi has nothing to say, so there is no use talking about it."[11] As a matter of fact, the sculptor was at that time out of hearing range of the audience; he was in the head of the Statue of Liberty, waiting for the signal to pull the flag covering his "daughter's face." This climax of the ceremony had been scheduled to take place immediately after William Evarts' speech in the name of the American Committee on the Statue of Liberty. A boy was supposed to give a signal to Bartholdi as soon as the speech was over so that the artist could do the unveiling. However, things did not work the way they had been planned. After being introduced by Scholfield, Evarts started his speech. He made a pause after his third paragraph, which ended with these words: "the indomitable will of the great sculptor Bartholdi." The signaler took this pause to be the end of the speech, and Bartholdi pulled the flag in through one of the openings of the Statue's crown. These openings are now glassed-in, so that visitors to the Statue may have a chance to look at the view of the harbor without being tempted to lean out, which might result in fatal accidents.

As soon as the Statue's face appeared completely, there was a shout: "Hail Liberty," and the people jumped to their feet cheering, forgetting the speaker. Naturally, Evarts was upset by all the noise. He turned his back to the enthusiastic audience and continued reading his speech to the President. As a senator he was later granted the privilege of having his speech printed. The enthusiasm on Bedloe's Island spread to the ships in the harbor, and there was a pandemonium of ships' horns in the fog which lasted a full fifteen minutes, disrupting the proceedings at the foot of the Statue of Liberty. The big bass whistles of the steamers and tugs contrasted with the piping tones of the little whistles of the yachts and the launches. There was one which had discovered very early that it had a knack for imitating the crow of a rooster, and it did not wait until the general uproar to make its shrill and malicious voice heard. It deserved being mentioned in the press as imitating the Gallic cock. There was also a salute by all the guns in the harbor.

After the noise had subsided, President Grover Cleveland made his acceptance speech. His strong and ringing voice could be heard clearly by everyone in the audience, and they all listened attentively when he said:

We will not forget that Liberty has made here her home, nor shall her chosen altar be neglected. Willing votaries will constantly keep alive its fires and these shall gleam upon the shores of our sister Republic in the East. Reflected thence and joined with answering rays, a stream of light shall pierce the darkness of ignorance and man's oppression until Liberty enlightens the world.[12]

The next speaker was A. Lefaivre, who was designated as Minister Plenipotentiary and Delegate Extraordinary from France. He wore the gorgeous coat with gold braids of the diplomatic representatives of his nation. Before speaking he removed his cocked hat and put a skull cap on his head. He spoke in English and ended his speech with these words:

Among the thousands of Europeans who are daily conveyed to these hospitable shores, no one will pass before this glorious emblem without immediately perceiving its moral greatness and without greeting it with respect and thankfulness.[13]

Back in the year 1875, when the appeal to the French people for the Statue of Liberty was launched, a distant relative of Liberty's creator, Amédée Bartholdi, was French Minister in Washington and gave support to the project. Had the Statue of Liberty been unveiled, as was hoped, at the time of the Centennial, there might have been three Bartholdis on Bedloe's Island...

After some music by the band, the Honorable Chauncey M. Depew, president of the Union League Club of New York, gave the commemorative address. Depew started by saying: "We dedicate this statue to the friendship of nations and the peace of the world."[14] The speech was rather long and contained many historical references, especially to Lafayette. One of the newspapers, which gave the address in full, wrote that in spite of its length "it held the closest attention of the audience throughout." Depew's address was followed by the Doxology: "Praise God from whom all blessings flow," played by the band. The audience was invited to sing as the band played.

After the benediction by the Right Reverend Henry C. Potter, an Episcopalian clergyman from New York, the assembly was dismissed. Then real trouble started. The proceedings had lasted longer than expected, and the people were in a hurry to get home — some of them to get ready for the big dinner at Delmonico's that night.

The policemen succeeded in keeping the crowd back long enough for the President to embark on a boat for the return to New York City. Then they gradually melted away, and there was a mad rush as if the people were afraid of being left behind to spend the night on the island. The crush was terrible. A gentleman exclaimed: "This is not merely disgraceful; it is positively outrageous!" Lesseps held

Tototte by the hand, endeavoring to shield her; the frightened girl was crying bitterly. The French delegates were pushed about. Some of them tried to take the whole affair humorously. One shouted: "La garde passe partout" (the guard passes everywhere), and another: "Place pour les députés" (Make room for the delegates).[15] The Reverends Potter and Storrs were jostled about until they nearly had their robes torn from their bodies. Chauncey Depew was seen helping Cornelius Vanderbilt whose nose was bleeding. Anyone who is familiar with the narrow passages and stairs leading from the area where the ceremony took place on Fort Wood to the exit from the fort can imagine how dangerous the situation was with the crowd pushing and struggling to get away. It was reported that several ladies were badly crushed. Well, had they not been warned to stay away from the ceremony?

Re-embarking was also a problem, with people not knowing on what boat their ticket would be accepted. The New York City aldermen got into the wrong boat, and the people who embarked on theirs ate all the food which had been prepared for those distinguished gentlemen. A newspaper reported that had not the crowd been composed of respectable people there might have been some serious accidents. According to a report in a French newspaper the ceremony ended in a terrible scuffle, "with the policemen not knowing their jobs."[16] Reports disagree as to how many policemen were on the island during the ceremony. There were supposed to be 250, and provisions had been made for a court to try possible offenders on the spot. Elsewhere we find that 200 particularly tall ones had been selected. The figure given in another account is 150, and a newspaper reporter stated that "their presence served rather to ornament the shores of the island than to preserve order."[17] Anyway, no arrests were made, and everyone finally got away including the main speaker, Chauncey M. Depew, who was left to find his way home as best he could. The author has not come across any specific reference as to how Auguste Bartholdi and his wife fared. Most likely they were pushed around like the others.

The American Committee on the Statue of Liberty later on had a special souvenir book of sixty-two pages printed to commemorate the great event of October 28. Its frontispiece is a reproduction of the invitation sent out for the ceremony. It contains much informa-

tion about the history of the Statue of Liberty such as the joint re-
solution by Congress to authorize the President of the United States
to set apart a site for the "colossal Statue of Liberty"; the texts of
speeches delivered at the unveiling ceremony; the names of the most
important people who were there; and the order of the proceedings,
with no reference of course to the disturbances which occurred during the ceremony and afterwards. A gilded quarto edition in a special
box was mailed to Bartholdi and is now at the *Musée Bartholdi* in
Colmar. It is accompanied by a letter addressed to him at his Paris
home, which reads:

My Dear Sir:

In response to the wishes of my colleagues of the Executive Committee,
I take great pleasure in presenting you on their behalf with a volume
descriptive of the inaugural ceremonies, occurring at the acceptance of
your great work "The Statue of Liberty" by the President and the People
of the United States on the 28th day of October, 1886.

This trifling souvenir illustrative of a memorable occasion, which was
made possible only by your Genius, as well as your heroic and untiring
efforts, only faintly represents the esteem in which your good name and
reputation are held by my associates, who take this occasion to renew the
assurances of their most distinguished consideration.

In which I pray you to include the affectionate regard of

Your faithful friend
Richard Butler
Secretary.

The Chamber of Commerce of New York State entertained at a
banquet at Delmonico's in New York City on the evening of the
unveiling. A little over two hundred gentlemen attended this function. President James M. Brown of the Chamber was the first to
enter the banquet hall with Ferdinand de Lesseps on his arm. The
honored guests sat on a raised platform. There was an orchestra in
the galleries of the hall, where several ladies sat. The menu, written
in French, had as hors d'oeuvres *Timbales à la De Lesseps,* as entrée
Côtelettes de Gelinottes à la Lafayette, and for dessert, printed in
large letters, *SORBET BARTHOLDI.*[18]

There were the usual speeches and toasts which are inseparable
from such great occasions and the guests went home only at one
o'clock the following morning. One of the toasts was to Bartholdi

and was written on the menu both in French and in English. It took its inspiration from the following ancient myth: "Jupiter had a severe headache; Vulcan opened his head with an axe; Minerva came forth fully armed."[19] Bartholdi replied in English, saying that someone had called him the Columbus of Bedloe's Island because none had discovered that island before him. He also said: "I do not take this reception for myself; I take it for my country — for France and for Alsace."[20] Bartholdi was presented with two white silk badges worn on the occasion of Lafayette's visit to America in 1824. Praises of Liberty came from all sides F. R. Coudert, a member of the American Committee on the Statue of Liberty, said in French that since the Sermon on the Mount, when the lesson of divine fraternity was heard, he knew of no doctrine comparable to that taught by the Statue of Liberty.[21]

While all this was going on at Delmonico's thousands of people were still waiting to see the fireworks which had been scheduled to start at 7 PM that night. The Battery and Brooklyn Bridge were crowded, and there were many crafts in the bay. Occasionally a light in the harbor was mistaken for Liberty's torch. However, weather conditions did not permit firework displays on that night, and the torch was not lit. When police finally gave assurance that there would be no fireworks, there was a mad rush for the elevated trains and other means of transportation. In some places, such as Brooklyn Bridge, no instructions were given to the policemen, and the people stayed there for a long time, waiting for the fireworks and the lighting of the torch. Among the incidents of that night reported in the press was that of young men forming lines on each side of a large puddle and laughing when people, thinking that there was a way open in the crowd, rushed into the water and mud.

October 28 was a day that the people of New York City and the vicinity were to remember for a long time. It has been mentioned that every year there is a ceremony at the Statue of Liberty to commemorate the unveiling. The ceremony of 1936, fiftieth anniversary of the dedication of the Statue, was particularly memorable. Mr. Richard, Mayor of Colmar and Mr. Netter, president of the *Théâtre Alsacien* of the city, came to New York, bringing with them many enlarged photographs of the rooms and exhibits in the *Musée Bartholdi,* as well as of Bartholdi's monuments in Colmar.[22] These pictures were framed; some of them are exhibited in the Administration Building at the Statue of Liberty with other pictures and items referring to the Statue, while the others are kept in a filing cabinet. Madame Netter, the widow of the gentleman who came to New York in 1936, and who is still living in Colmar, told this author that her husband and the Mayor had quite a bit of trouble passing through the American customs a wreath of fir branches from Alsace which they had brought to place at the foot of the great work by a son of Colmar.

While the ceremony at the Statue of Liberty is now a tradition, nothing is done to reenact the great land and naval parades. Maybe some day the unveiling of the Statue of Liberty will also be commemorated as "Bartholdi Day" or "Liberty Day" with a parade on Fifth Avenue and maybe a legal holiday. While New York City's population has increased greatly since 1886, and while its composition has changed quite a bit, some of the organizations which paraded in 1886 are still in existence today. Even some of the participants may still be alive, such as the little girls that marched with the Grand Army of the Republic and presented flowers and a banner to Bartholdi. The life span is very long these days. In this connection, this author likes to remember that either in 1951 or in 1954, on one of the two occasions he was called upon to speak on Bartholdi at the ceremony organized at the Statue of Liberty by *L' Union Alsacienne* and the Central Committee of the French-Speaking Societies of New York, an elderly gentleman approached him after his talk and told him that when he was a little school boy in France he had given ten centimes for Liberty when money was being raised for the Statue.[23]

CHAPTER TEN

Bartholdi and the United States After the Unveiling of the Statue of Liberty

After the unveiling of the Statue of Liberty, receptions and dinners followed one another for Bartholdi and the French delegates, with Ferdinand de Lesseps being particularly feted. The Chamber of Commerce of New York State had organized a special reception in his honor in the afternoon of October 29. However, he was unable to accept an invitation he had received to go to Montreal as guest of the great Canadian city. Cyrus Field also entertained him. Levi P. Morton who had been closely connected with the beginnings of the Statue of Liberty in France and who had received it in the name of his country, invited Bartholdi to dinner on October 29. Among the guests was Léon Meunier, editor of the *Courrier des Etats Unis*.[1]

Madame Bartholdi in Colmar was kept informed of all the happenings in the United States. Back in Hoffman House, after a trip to Niagara Falls in a special palace car as guests of the Union League Club and the New York Central Railroad, Jeanne Bartholdi wrote to her mother-in-law a glowing letter about the thrilling experiences she and her husband had had during the previous few days:

Auguste is feeling fine. His dear face is shining with pleasure. What enthusiasm! What a triumph! . . . Our dear Auguste has been feted like a monarch. We can be proud: you to be his mother, and I to be his wife.

How happy I am to see Auguste so justly rewarded after so much labor!
In one day he saw the whole population hail him; in every mouth was
the name Bartholdi.[2]

About the trip to Niagara Falls she wrote that crowds were waiting
at each railroad station to see Bartholdi and to cheer him, and that
in one locality where the train was not supposed to stop, the inhabitants made the train halt and Auguste had to get out of the
railroad carriage to shake all hands. She concluded:

For the time being the name Bartholdi is on all lips in America. I hope
that this will have a repercussion in France, and that they will know how
to appreciate what Auguste has done for his country, as an artist and as
a patriot.[3]

While at Niagara Falls the French group stayed at Spencer House,
a hotel open the whole year. In a letter to his mother Bartholdi
complained that he had the whole French delegation constantly on
his arms; at any moment one of them would come to disturb him for
the slightest reason. Ferdinand de Lesseps and most of the other
French delegates sailed away on *La Gascogne* on November 6. The
ship's lounge was full of roses for the farewell party which was attended by Bartholdi and his wife.

After the unveiling of the Statue of Liberty quite a bit was found
in the newspapers about the monument and its meaning, such as:

The Statue of Liberty symbolizes the peaceful life of freedom of two
mighty nations. . . The hand of the great sculptor who wrought it has
given palpable embodiment to the best hopes of mankind, but the word
for which it stands will be heard in triumph long after this enduring
bronze has crumbled into dust.[4]

Two days after the unveiling another American newspaper commented on America's obligations to make liberty known to others
"our Indian and Chinese experiences notwithstanding," and added
that "our idea of liberty may not yet have taken on its final and
perfect form."[5] A French newspaper wrote: "Our nation is cordially
dined and feasted, and, for the time being at least, the two republics
are truly sisters."[6] *The World,* which was of course still in the fore-
front for everything concerning Liberty, wrote that the Statue of
Liberty would be an encouragement to other nations to win their

freedom. This newspaper also reported that *The Times* of London had commented sarcastically on the unveiling of the "French Goddess of Liberty," stating that Bartholdi had wanted to avoid oblivion by making a better statue than that of the German national hero Arminius, and that Liberty would nearly, but not quite, reach the top of Nelson's Column on Trafalgar Square in London. Throughout the campaign for the Pedestal of the Statue of Liberty, *The World* had occasionally referred to unfavorable comments by English newspapers. In those days the British and the French were rivals in Africa. No representative from Great Britain and, for that matter, none from Germany, attended any of the October 28 celebrations.

According to the press work continued on the Statue of Liberty for some time after the unveiling. Once again pigmy men were seen hanging down from the neck and the shoulders of the gigantic woman, hammering and polishing. The stairway inside the Statue was being completed, and visitors were prohibited from going into the Statue because there was still danger of rivets and small pieces of metal falling on the people's heads.

The repeatedly postponed great night of fireworks and the lighting of the Statue finally took place on November 1. At 7 PM a bomb shot was heard on Bedloe's Island. This was the signal for the ships in the harbor to sound their horns as the light of the torch appeared. There were projectors all around the Pedestal, but only the lower part of the Statue was floodlit. A bewildering succession of rockets, bombs, fiery serpents, sparkling geysers, and shooting stars lightened the sky above the harbor. The climax was a huge circle of colored lights at the base of the Statue which lit Liberty's face for a short time. Bartholdi was not back from his trip to Niagara Falls when this great display took place, but it was possible for him to see the Statue as it was normally lighted at that time. Among the suggestions he made was that of putting colored glass in the windows of the crown, so that the colors red, blue, and white would appear. He also asked if it would be possible to make the Statue look brighter than the Pedestal. This is how it looks today, and the torch is provided with sufficient candle power to shine brightly.

People who cross New York harbor today on the Staten Island ferryboat or who look at Liberty from the shore take the lighting of the Statue of Liberty for granted. They do not realize how much red

156

tape was involved until the monument was even faintly lighted. It took some time to find out who was responsible for the lighting, and this found an echo in the press. On November 14, the same day as *The World* announced the departure of Bartholdi and his wife, it published a picture of Liberty with her torch extinguished and embarrassed by the many ribbons of red tape.

Under the title of "Farewell in tears," the newspaper published a short article about the artist's departure. Bartholdi had planned to stay in the United States until the end of November, but bad news about his mother's health obliged him to change his plans and to cancel a number of public appearances. He sailed on *La Bourgogne* on November 13. Since the ship was to leave early Saturday morning the Bartholdis' friends went to see them off on board the steamer on Friday night. A reporter from *The World,* however, went to see the artist early on the morning of the departure. The sculptor came out to meet him, wearing a heavy coat with its collar upturned and warming his hands in his pockets. As though he foresaw dimly what the future was to hold for him, Bartholdi left this message with the reporter: "My farewell to the American people is good-bye in tears."[7]

After its creator's departure from the United States in November 1886, some time passed before the Statue of Liberty became the well looked after shrine that it is today. At present the island and Bartholdi's Statue form a National Monument under the supervision of the National Park Service, which is a part of the United States Department of the Interior. The entire island is used for services connected with the Monument, and Bedloe's Island has been renamed Liberty Island as Bartholdi liked to call it. The American Museum of Immigration has been constructed lately on the island below the Statue's Pedestal. AMI is now located there because of the great symbolic meaning the Statue of Liberty has acquired for countless immigrants and descendants of immigrants to the United States. However, this was not always so. The Army did not get out of the island in a hurry, and at one time there was a plan to locate a sanitarium there. In a letter to Butler, written in 1890, Bartholdi expressed his relief that the idea had been given up. He added:

My idea has always been that it would be in the future a kind of Pantheon for the glories of American Independence; that you would build around the monument the statues of your great men and collect there all the noble memories. This island should become a sort of pilgrimage, a charming walk for the City.[8]

The Statue of Liberty is becoming more and more as Bartholdi visualized it. Many New Yorkers visit it when the weather is pleasant.

It is not this author's concern to report on all the phases Liberty went through until it could properly be spoken of as "enlightening the World," until the National Park Service finally obtained control of the whole island and could make a park out of it, or until it became the great symbol it now is — familiar to all, appearing on stamps, and many other items. Some of this story can be found in a number of publications. The author's concern in the rest of this chapter will be with Bartholdi's relationship with America after Liberty's unveiling. This information is not well known, and the artist's personal papers throw a new light on Liberty's creator. It is unfortunate that this light is not always as good as one would like it to be.

Although the triumph and elation surrounding the unveiling of the Statue of Liberty, when the name Bartholdi was on all lips, could naturally not last forever, one would like to imagine that the great sculptor, after reaching the goal of so many years of painstaking work, would be able to lead a peaceful existence, surrounded by honors, with no financial worries, and not having to bother with things which appear so minor when considering the magnitude of his achievement. Unfortunately this was not the case due to a combination of circumstances.

The sculptor's first setback was the necessity of having to return to France two weeks early because of his mother's illness. Because of this he was unable to capitalize fully on the great success of the unveiling to obtain good commissions for dollar-paid works in the United States, and when he tried to arrange this and other things by mail, the results disappointed him. His mother died only in 1891, but her failing health was a constant worry to her son and often hampered his activities. He did not return to the United States until after her death.

Bartholdi had not asked for, nor received, a commission for designing the Statue of Liberty and for all his labor in connection with this project, which probably would never have materialized without his tireless efforts. It was mentioned earlier in this work that the sculptor had sunk quite a bit of his own money — about twenty thousand dollars, he claimed — into the project. The artist, however, was hoping that his talent would be recognized — first, through awards: second, through many reproductions of the Statue for which he would get a certain income since the work was patented; third, that he would get the opportunity to make other monuments for which he would get commissions. After all his profession was to create statues and monuments and he could not be expected to continue working without remuneration. In the first respect, he did not appear to be quite satisfied with what he got; in the second, he was to be greatly disappointed; while in the third, he was to appear at times in a rather undignified position because of overconfidence or miscaculations. One cannot help feeling sorry for him because of this.

It is already known that Bartholdi received a silver globe surmounted by a hand holding a torch, made at Tiffany's, New York, from Joseph Pulitzer and *The World,* as a remembrance of the campaign of 1885. However, he was hoping for more from America. In a letter to Pulitzer, dated Colmar, October 13, 1887, nearly a year after the unveiling of Liberty, the artist unloaded his heart to his American friend. A rough copy of this letter with corrections by Mr. Creuse, his English teacher, is to be found among his private papers in Colmar. He wrote:

Last year much was spoken about American gratitude towards me. It was said that Congress would vote me an award (corrected by teacher as "acknowledgement") in consideration of all the great sacrifices which I have had to bear; afterwards a monument was spoken of, for which I was to receive an order, and so forth. All that is over; the Americans have done nothing for me; it is only through you that I got a souvenir in the shape of the beautiful testimonial presented by *The World.*[9]

After giving vent to his displeasure at not being commissioned to erect the Lafayette Monument in front of the White House in Washington, and complaining about the ingratitude of the people and the unfairness of the selecting committee, the sculptor requested that Pulitzer "keep my letter to yourself alone because I wish not to show my feelings except to a friend like yourself."[10] Maybe Bartholdi expected a vote of thanks from Congress that would have enhanced his prestige. As far as Pulitzer was concerned, the sculptor was to overestimate the newspaper man's friendship towards him, as will be seen further on.

In a letter to Butler, Bartholdi expressed concern at not receiving any diploma showing that he had received the Freedom of the City of New York. It has been mentioned that this illuminated parchment is hanging in the *Musée Bartholdi* in Colmar. The frame bears the inscription: October 27, 1887. He must, therefore, have received it about one year after the event, probably after an inquiry by one of his American friends. The artist considered all such things important, and he probably hung it in his studio in Paris, just as dentists and other professional people like to display their framed degrees. It must be said, however, that many of the awards received by Bartholdi, including the ones received at the Philadelphia Centennial are in Colmar, not in frames, but in folders.

The artist also expected some recognition from France for the erection of the Statue of Liberty, a monument to Franco-American friendship — not only for himself but for his American collaborators. The French government had agreed to send vases from the porcelain factory of Sèvres to Pulitzer, Butler, and a few others. Butler got his, but others were delayed, or not sent according to instructions. The minister who had promised the gifts was no longer in office. . .

As far as Bartholdi was concerned, he had been made a Commander in the Legion of Honor in December 1886. This decoration was seldom awarded, but it appears that the sculptor was after more than that, maybe after a well-paid contract for some great monument. Anyway, he asked Butler to send him one of the souvenir programs of the unveiling of Liberty "nicely bound in the American style (*Chic Américain*) with an official dedication from your committee to be presented to our President of the Republic."[11] It has been pointed out previously that the American Committee on the Statue of Liberty had issued such a souvenir program and that Bartholdi had received one which is now in Colmar. The artist wanted one for the French President in order to further attract his attention, following the old proverb: God helps him who helps himself. The French artist added in his letter: "I shall, later on, explain

160

to you why this manifestation from the Committee to the President might be useful to me to bring our government to grant me some favors respecting the Statue."[12]

Bartholdi did not hesitate to use his American connections to further his aims in France. The lawsuit in which he had become engaged in order to prevent the City of Paris from condemning his property continued after his return from the unveiling of Liberty. When he saw that there was nothing much he could do about it, in spite of his being a famous artist, he wanted at least to get as much as he could for the condemned property, and in 1892 he asked Butler to write a letter stating that the lawsuit had obliged him to stay in Paris and had made him miss profitable contracts in the United States.[13] It was true that he had intended going to the United States, his mother's death the year before having removed the main obstacle to distant traveling. The contracts, however, were only in his imagination, as he was to find out when he did travel to the United States the following year, in 1893.

The courts awarded a substantial amount of money to Bartholdi for the loss of his home and studio, and the inconvenience resulting from the move. He settled in a house close by, on Assas Street, overlooking the Luxembourg Gardens. There was no great publicity about Bartholdi's last visit to the United States, and the artist was no doubt saddened to see that his "daughter Liberty" was not yet properly cared for. Although the artist knew that the welcome received in 1886 could not be repeated, he was hoping to get more out of his trip, and he expressed his discouragement in a letter to Butler:

I feel gratified, dear friend, by all the trouble which you take for me, but I am particularly moved by the feeling which it expresses towards me. You are the single man who thinks of all the pecuniary sacrifices which I have made formerly and of the hard times I had to cross: nobody in America as you has ever thought of trying to repair my old wounds.[14]

Another disappointment that Bartholdi was to have in regard to America concerned his patent rights. It has been mentioned that at the time of his second visit to the United States, in 1876, he had obtained a copyright in Washington for the Statue of Liberty. Court actions to prevent people from imitating the Statue of Liberty started as soon as the monument was completed. On October 25, 1886 an injunction was obtained restraining Joseph Perrin from making and selling badges bearing the likeness of the Statue of Liberty.[15] A few days later another injunction was granted against Godfrey Rossberg restraining him from manufacturing and selling bronze imitations of the Statue. It has been seen that quite a number of such items was already in the hands of men who peddled them on October 28. Bartholdi, who was not getting any commission for designing Liberty, was hoping that he would derive some income from royalties coming from the reproduction of the statue, as is shown by a letter he wrote to his friend Glaenzer in 1883:

I have some little hope that there may be a demand for the same (the models) which may help to make up for the large sacrifices that, as you personally so well know, had to be made by me.[16]

The hope was "little" indeed, as it was eventually impossible to prevent the reproduction of the Statue of Liberty. As long as the Statue was not completed the artist put any royalties accruing from the sale of models into the general fund.

Bartholdi's main trouble was with the "terrible Brundage," his licensee in the United States, and there is a considerable amount of correspondence about this matter. Originally Bartholdi had granted to the French firm Avoiron the sole right to reproduce the Statue of Liberty, and there are some Avoiron reproductions in the United States. Later on, thinking probably that it would be more profitable to have the Statue reproduced in the United States because of the larger market, the artist approved the sale of this right to the American firm Brundage. However, there was an omission in the documents when the patent was transferred, and Bartholdi signed the papers which had been translated into English without noticing that Article VI was missing. This article read as follows:

The property of these rights of reproduction has been granted to Messrs. Avoiron and Co. under the condition of their paying to Mr. Bartholdi, or his legal representatives, as a royalty, ten per centum of the net price of each copy issued. Messrs. Brundage and Co. agree to assume said charges towards Mr. Bartholdi; they shall send acknowledgement of the same to Messrs. Avoiron and Co. and to Mr. Bartholdi who, under said conditions, is consenting to the transfer made by Messrs. Avoiron and Co. within the limits above laid down.[17]

Bartholdi, referring to the omission of this very important article in a letter to Butler, admitted that he should have read the papers more carefully before signing them. He regretted being so "short-minded in business matters," and hoped that Brundage would understand the situation and return the contract so that article VI could be included. This was in August 1886, quite a while before the completion of the re-erection of Liberty in her permanent abode, and there were reasons to hope that the matter could be settled in due course. At that time the sculptor was much more concerned with the membership of the French delegation to the unveiling ceremony and anxious that all should get invitations.

After Bartholdi's return to France and his being occasionally short of cash, this matter of patent rights became more important. He sent a power-of-attorney to Butler in November 1886. But things did not work the right way, and by 1889 he appeared to have given up all hopes when he wrote to his friend Butler: "I think it is not possible to do more on behalf of my interest with Brundage. It is impossible for me to purchase the stock. It is a pity, but I prefer to give up the matter."[18] In the same letter the sculptor wrote about the expenses he had incurred to have a work of art ready for the 1889 Exhibition in Paris, and about "the charges which my dear daughter Liberty has left to me, and the misfortunes which occurred to me since that time."[19]

Among the misfortunes to which Bartholdi alluded was that of not having been commissioned to make the Lafayette monument in Washington, and he attempted to make up for this.[20] There seemed to be an opportunity in 1887, when the author of a magazine article stated that there was some talk in the United States of offering a statue of Washington to France. This statue of the great American president was to be a token of appreciation for the gift of the Statue of Liberty. The writer of the article added that there existed a bronze reproduction of the Washington statue by the French sculptor Houdon, and a suggestion was made that the United States acquire this work of art and offer it to the Louvre Museum in Paris. The present owner of the statue was willing to sell it for 40,000 francs. This article was brought to the attention of Joseph Pulitzer who got the idea to purchase the statue himself and present it to France. Pulitzer asked G. W. Turner, manager of *The World*, to approach Bartholdi about forming a committee to take charge of the affair and to announce the gift on the occasion of the dinner to be given in Paris on October 28, in celebration of the first anniversary of the unveiling of the Statue of Liberty.[21] Strangely enough a letter from Bartholdi crossed the message from Pulitzer. The French artist offered to make a monument representing Lafayette and Washington for the same purpose as Pulitzer had in mind for the amount of $37,000. The sculptor added: "In what concerns me, you may understand how delighted I would be to take my revenge."[22] He was naturally thinking of those who had prevented him from having a monument in front of the White House. He then proposed that a subscription be started by *The World* to raise the $37,000, and suggested that the monument be presented in 1889, on the occasion of the celebration of the hundredth anniversary of the beginning of the French Revolution. He added that such a subscription would be easy. Pulitzer immediately cabled back: "Public subscription impossible now. You can only count on my own forty thousand francs. That is the limit of my responsibility. Letter by next steamer."[23]

Bartholdi, however, knowing that Pulitzer was very well-off — he was to die a multimillionaire — mistakenly believed that his great friend would give more than the 40,000 francs. This seems to be indicated by the rough copy of a speech which he planned to give at the anniversary dinner of Liberty's unveiling. Lafayette and Washington were to be the central figures, and some others were to be added around the pedestal.[24] The artist had overestimated Pulitzer's generosity, and he was to be set right by the letter from Turner, which he received a few days later, stating that Mr. Pulitzer's first idea had been to purchase the Houdon statue for 40,000 francs, then "upon second consideration, he decided to offer you the opportunity, if you chose to accept it, to make an entirely new statue for the above sum."[25] This was rather humiliating for the creator of the world's largest statue, but in spite of this warning Bartholdi undertook a project which was to cost more.

While the artist was working on this new monument he found out that a certain Mr. Evans, an American resident of Paris, wanted to offer a statue of Lafayette to the City of Paris. Feeling that such a gift might spoil the effect of the presentation of the monument that he was preparing, he decided to write a letter to the President of the

164

Municipal Council of Paris, the rough copy of which is among his papers, suggesting that Mr. Evans be dissuaded from making this gift at this time for the sake of Mr. Pulitzer and, although he did not say so, for his own sake as the sculptor of the monument.[26]

There is a large amount of correspondence about Bartholdi's Lafayette and Washington monument as well as bills and receipts. Joseph Pulitzer started sending money by instalments. In November 1891 another 25,000 francs was still needed to make up the balance, and Bartholdi, who had to pay 27,000 francs cash to the founder Barbedienne, asked for the 25,000 in a letter in which he said that he had had many expenses in connection with his mother's recent death.[27] These probably included expenses for a funerary monument. At the time of this letter Pulitzer was suffering from ill health and had eye trouble. He was taking trips to see specialists, and had just taken a trip to Europe, so the matter was not settled until the following year while Bartholdi was worrying lest the founder would decide to scrap the statues. Bartholdi had more headaches about his Lafayette and Washington group, including that of having the monument transported by the City of Paris — that was receiving it as a gift — until it was finally erected on the Square of the United States in Paris, where it still stands. There is a plaque on it with the date of 1895, and an inscription which says that it was a gift to the City of Paris from Joseph Pulitzer. The newspaper owner expressed regret that such a location had been selected. He would have preferred that this monument would not have been located in a district which he thought was largely populated by American residents. This monument is now surrounded by trees and park benches on which mothers sit while their small children are playing.

It turned out that the Lafayette and Washington monument was a disappointment to both Pulitzer and Bartholdi. The former had originally intended to make a gift to the French people, not just to the City of Paris, while the latter would have liked to have created a much more significant monument, worthy of the donor's intention.

An exact replica of the monument was placed in New York at the corner of Manhattan Avenue and 114th Street, near Morningside Park. The inscription says that it was presented to the City of New York by Charles B. Rouss in 1900. Bartholdi was still alive at that time, and had the satisfaction of hearing that another of his monuments had been unveiled in the New World. The presentation was made on April 19, "Patriot's Day," commemorating the 125th anniversary of the Battle of Lexington and the 123rd anniversary of the arrival of General Lafayette in America. The ceremony took place at Carnegie Hall, in New York. The program included a reading by the American poet Edwin Markham of his poem "Our Deathless Dead." There is no doubt that Bartholdi was eulogized in some of the addresses which were given on that day.[28]

If he saw the monument today Auguste Bartholdi would be saddened at the sight of all the scribblings by people from the neighborhood which deface the monument's base. On the other hand, if he traveled to Liberty Island he would, no doubt, be very pleased to see the great reverence which now surrounds his "daughter Liberty" which has acquired in the eyes of the people of America and of the whole world a significance of which its creator did not dream, and which he would have probably considered an ample reward for his many efforts.

Epilogue

In addition to the Lafayette and Washington of Paris and New York Auguste Bartholdi was to create many more monuments which were unveiled after Liberty. Some of them were in his home town; others in various parts of France and in countries close to France. Among his Colmar works was the statue of the Alsatian scientist Adolphe Hirn whom he modeled sitting in an armchair atop his pedestal, seeming to ponder over some problem. Hirn's widow sent him a letter of appreciation. The artist must have been particularly pleased with the following passage of this letter:

You have succeeded in idealizing and in bringing out what is most difficult to render in the face of my beloved husband: his air of great kindness, of subtlety, of depth; in short you have found this something, this reflection of the soul which became year after year more accentuated and gave him a particular impression which attracted all hearts.[1]

Bartholdi continued to represent France's great men. He made a monument to Gambetta, the statesman, in the latter's home town. Also his big statue of Vercingétorix was finally unveiled more than thirty years after it was conceived. The transportation of this large statue from Paris to Clermont-Ferrand in the central part of France was witnessed by many.

Not very far from the railroad station of Basle, Switzerland, stands another monument by Bartholdi belonging to the period following the unveiling of the Statue of Liberty. This monument commemorates the help given by Switzerland to the city of Strasbourg, Alsace, during the Franco-Prussian War. There is no doubt that this war and its consequences were among the dominant influences on Bartholdi's career. No less than ten of his monuments, including the two best known — the Statue of Liberty and the Lion of Belfort — probably would never have seen the light if it had not been for this war and the way Bartholdi was affected by it as a son of Alsace.

It has been pointed out on more than one occasion that Bartholdi's conception of art was criticized by some of his American colleagues;

therefore it will be interesting to hear an explanation of his feeling for art given towards the end of his life. The occasion was a speech given in 1898 at the annual distribution of awards at the *Lycée Louis-le-Grand,* his alma mater, in Paris. The sculptor said:

The artist is a man of impression; analysis is for him an effort which hampers his intuition. . . The act of creating works of painting or sculpture is certainly art in its specific meaning, but the general meaning of the word art is this feeling for the ideal which comes to you from all good and beautiful things — from nature, from life, from the works of the spirit. It was here that I first received this generous and productive feeling which elevates the soul.[2]

Until shortly before his death the artist worked on his own funeral monument which represented an allegorical figure holding out a laurel wreath. Bartholdi knew that he was suffering from an incurable lung ailment, which developed about three years before his death and showed violent symptoms during the last few months of his life. As the end drew near he was only breathing in gasps.[3] He died on the morning of October 4, 1904, at the end of a night-long vigil by his wife and friends; he was seventy years old.

Newspapers in Europe and America published accounts of his life and work with a number of errors, as was to be expected. President Theodore Roosevelt sent a telegram to his widow, expressing the sympathy of the American people. A New York newspaper reported that Bartholdi died poor and that the indemnity he had received for his condemned property on Vavin Street was about "the only resource that enabled him to live in comfort."[4] This was probably going a little too far. There is no doubt that the Bartholdi family fortune had been depleted over the years as a result of the death of the artist's father when he and his brother were still small children, shortly after which the family went to Paris where the two children were educated. Also Bartholdi made several trips abroad paying all expenses himself for some of them. Moreover he was an artist and often created sculptures, just for the love of art, which he gave to his home town or elsewhere. He never recovered the more than $20,000 which he had sunk in the Statue of Liberty project. However, in spite of all this, when he died he left substantial real estate in Alsace, in addition to the home which is now the *Musée*

Bartholdi in Colmar, to which the contents of Bartholdi's studio and the furnishings of his home in Paris were transferred after the death of his widow which occurred some years later. There were various bequests, including one to help with the upkeep of the old Colmar home.

The sculptor's funeral was an imposing ceremony on October 7, attended by hundreds of people, with a military honor guard participating in it. The body was laid to rest at the Montparnasse Cemetery where Bartholdi's beloved mother, who had been an inspiration to him for so many years, was already resting in peace. Newspapers wrote that among the mourners were many of Bartholdi's models and students. This may have been so, although he never referred in the correspondence which the author has come across to models or to his teaching sculpture.

The speeches delivered at the artist's funeral were printed in a booklet.[5] Although the United States embassy was represented at the funeral, there is no speech by any American representative in the booklet, as one might have expected. Reverend Roberty, the minister who officiated, said:

At first it must perhaps be stated that Bartholdi was above all a *believer,* not in the dogmatic and restricted meaning of this word, but in its broadest meaning, that is at the same time its most intimate and truest meaning. Beyond the forms of the visible world, he believed in an absolute and living beauty which human works can reproduce only imperfectly. . . It was the soul of France, of her freedom-loving spirit, rather than an artistic conception which inspired the colossal statue of *Liberty Enlightening the World,* and which animated his work and his active life.[6]

Mr. Fleury, who represented the Association of French artists, of which Bartholdi had been the vice president, spoke about the meaning of Liberty whose first model was made out of clay from France and which was to symbolize what the French Revolution had given to humanity on the threshold of "the great republic that we have helped to liberate."[7]

Mr. Kiener, a leading Colmar textile manufacturer, had come to represent Bartholdi's home town, which his many monuments had helped to make "one of the most beautiful jewels" among the cities of Alsace, and to which he had returned so often to stay in the old family home.

The city of Colmar was later to commission the sculptor Louis-Noël to make a statue of her illustrious son. It still stands in one of Colmar's loveliest parks. Auguste Bartholdi in bronze is represented leaning on an easel which supports a small model of Liberty Enlightening the World. It is the author's hope that some day a replica of this work will rise on Liberty Island, so that the gigantic Statue's torch may also lighten the likeness of its creator.

Sources

BARTHOLDIANA COLLECTIONS

FRANCE

Letters from Auguste Bartholdi to his mother. They were classified by Madame Bartholdi and are kept in her former home in Colmar — now the *Musée Bartholdi.* In the notes and references the designation used is — *Letters from Auguste.*

Madame Bartholdi's personal papers, other than letters from her son. These include an incredible variety of items, such as rough copies of letters to her son, newspapers, telegrams, announcements, invitations, postcards, and many souvenirs carefully preserved by her. They are in the *Musée Bartholdi* which is abbreviated as MBC in the notes and references.

Musée Bartholdi, Colmar. Under this heading are included numerous items, such as awards, letters, and other material not included under the two previous headings.

Bibliothèque Municipale, Colmar. This collection includes transcripts of letters, newspapers, and pamphlets, some of which are not available elsewhere.

Conservatoire National des Arts et Métiers, Paris. This institution is both a museum and a school. In its library the artist's widow deposited a very interesting collection. This collection includes the clippings received by Bartholdi from clipping agencies, particularly the *Argus de la Presse* and personal papers such as invitations to functions and menus. Among the museum's exhibits is a diorama of the Statue of Liberty. The reason why all these items are there is because the museum's curator was a friend of the Bartholdis. Material in this collection is designated as — *Argus.*

UNITED STATES

New York Historical Society, New York City. This interesting collection contains largely material concerning the activities of the American Committee on the Statue of Liberty, as well as press clippings. The abbreviation used is — NYHS.

New York Public Library, New York City. There is valuable material on the Statue of Liberty and Bartholdi in several divisions of the library. The most useful to the author has been the large number of letters received by Richard Butler, Secretary of the American Committee on the Statue of Liberty, and by others. These are given in the notes and references with their dates. Other information obtained from the collections is designated by the abbreviation NYPL.

Library of Congress, Washington D.C. Some items from this collection were exhibited in 1954 on the occasion of the 120th anniversary of Bartholdi's birth and the 50th anniversary of his death.

BOOKS, PAMPHLETS, AND ARTICLES WITH AUTHORS, GIVEN IN THE ORDER IN WHICH THEY APPEAR FOR THE FIRST TIME IN THE NOTES AND REFERENCES

Rice, A.Th., *The Statue of Liberty Enlightening the World, described by the Sculptor Bartholdi,* New York, 1885.

Bruxer, J., "Der Colmarer Bildhauer Auguste Bartholdi plannte vor 100 Jahren ein Riensendenkmal für das Suez Kanal," *Le Nouveau-Rhin Français,* Colmar, November 29, 1959.

Koenig, P. E., "Bartholdi et l'Amérique," *La Vie en Alsace,* Strasbourg, 1934.

Bartholdi, A. *L'Album du Bord,* Paris, 1879.

Exposition Internationale de Philadelphie en 1876. Section Française. Rapport sur les Arts Décoratifs par. M. Auguste Bartholdi, membre du jury international, Paris. 1877.

Ch. Lefèbre, "L'Oeuvre de Bartholdi," *Revue Alsacienne,* Paris, 1881.

Ch. Blanc, *Les artistes de mon temps,* Paris, 1876.

L. Giclas, *Album of Light,* Washington, 1924.

Completion of the Mammoth Statue of Liberty Enlightening the World, Banquet given by Mr. Henry Gillig in honor of M. Auguste Bartholdi, the sculptor, Wednesday Evening, May 21, 1884.

Inauguration of the Statue of Liberty Enlightening the World by the President of the United States, 1887.

Discours prononcés le vendredi, 7 octobre, 1904, aux obsèques de F. A. Bartholdi, 1904.

PERIODICALS PUBLISHED IN FRANCE, GIVEN IN THE ORDER OF FIRST APPEARANCE IN NOTES AND REFERENCES.

Le Nouveau-Rhin Français, Colmar
Le Monde Illustré, Paris
Journal Illustré, Paris
La France, Paris
L'Industriel Alsacien, Mulhouse
Le Petit Journal, Paris
Mouvement Scientifique
Le Siècle, Paris
Le Temps, Paris
Le Soleil, Paris
Le Monde, Paris
Le Petit Temps, Paris

PERIODICALS PUBLISHED IN THE UNITED STATES, GIVEN IN THE ORDER OF FIRST APPEARANCE IN NOTES AND REFERENCES.@

Harper's Weekly, New York.
Daily Graphic, New York.
Courrier des Etats-Unis, New York.
Star, Long Island City.
New York Daily Tribune, New York.
Evening Telegram, New York.
Press, Philadelphia.
Irish World, New York.
New York Times, New York.
Evening Post, New York.
Boston Daily Globe, Boston.
World, New York.
Coney Island News, New York.
Chicago Tribune, Chicago.
New York Herald, New York.
Independent, New York.
Morning Journal, New York.
Frank Leslie Illustrated Newspaper, New York.

@ *Note* Articles have been omitted in front of periodicals published in the United States.

Notes and References

PROLOGUE

1. When the author visited the *Musée Bartholdi* during the summer of 1965, he noticed that the models had been removed. He was told that only some of them would be put back, because the space was needed for temporary exhibits.
2. This clause in the will is still respected. The present honorary curator, Mr. Pierre Burger, a local judge, is a Protestant.

CHAPTER I

1. MBC.
2. Library of Congress, Washington, D.C.
3. *Letters from Auguste,* October 16, 1864.
4. MBC.
5. *Letters from Auguste,* November 6, 1869.
6. Madame Bartholdi to Charles, rough copy of unfinished letter, November 1864.
7. MBC.
8. The fountain is floodlit at night during the summer as are many of Colmar's tourist attractions.
9. A. Th. Rice, *The Statue of Liberty Enlightening the World, described by the Sculptor Bartholdi,* New York, 1885, p. 14. Laboulaye's name is often to be found written without the *de* in front of it.
10. *Letters from Auguste,* March 23, 1869.
11. *Ibid.,* April 15, 1869.
12. *Ibid.,* April 26, 1869.
13. *Ibid.,* December 16, 1869.
14. *Ibid.,* December 20, 1869.
15. Rice, *op. cit.,* p. 37.
16. *Argus.*
17. *Ibid.*

18. Joseph Bruxer, "Der Colmarer Bildhauer Auguste Bartholdi plannte vor 100 Jahren ein Riesendenkmal für das Suez Kanal," *Le Nouveau Rhin Français,* Colmar, November 29, 1959.
19. Rice, *op. cit.,* p. 19.
20. Edmond About to Bartholdi, La Schlitt, October 13, 1868.
21. *Letters from Auguste,* November 14, 1869.
22. *Ibid.,* December 27, 1869.

CHAPTER II

1. MBC.
2. *Letters from Auguste,* Paris, June 2, 1870.
3. *Ibid.,* Tours., November 13, 1870.
4. Rice, *op. cit.,* p. 15.
5. Event with date recorded by Madame Bartholdi on one of the envelopes containing letters from her son.
6. Rice, *op. cit.,* pp. 16-17.
7. Paul-Ernest Koenig, "Bartholdi et l'Amérique," *La Vie en Alsace,* Strasbourg, 1934, p. 171.
8. *Ibid.,* p. 172.
9. *Ibid.*
10. Madame Bartholdi to Auguste, Colmar, June 24, 1871.
11. Koenig, *op. cit.,* p. 171.

174

12. *Ibid.*, p. 172.
13. Madame Bartholdi to Auguste, Colmar, August 2, 1871.
14. *Ibid.*, August 13, 1871.
15. Koenig, *op. cit.*, p. 175.
16. *Ibid.*, p. 173.
17. *Ibid.*
18. *Ibid.*
19. *Ibid.* p. 175.
20. *Letters from Auguste,* Paris, December 16, 1871.
21. The presence of this bust in New York City was brought to this author's attention by Dr. Walter Pitkin, an historian who resided on Liberty Island.

CHAPTER III

1. MBC.
2. Charles Blanc to Madame Bartholdi, Paris, March 31, 1873.
3. *Le Monde Illustré,* Paris, May 9, 1874.
4. MBC.
5. Rice, *op. cit.*, pp. 52-53.
6. NYPL.
7. *Journal Illustré,* Paris, November 21, 1875.
8. MBC.
9. *Harper's Weekly,* November 27, 1875.
10. MBC.
11. *Ibid.*
12. The American Committee on the Statue of Liberty.
13. Auguste Bartholdi, *L'Album du Bord,* Paris, 1879.
14. *Daily Graphic,* New York, June 2, 1876.
15. See above, Bartholdiana Collections.
16. *Letters from Auguste,* Philadelphia, June 6, 1876.
17. *Ibid.*, June 14, 1876.

18. *Courrier des Etats-Unis,* New York, June 10, 1876.
19. *Ibid.*, June 13, 1876.
20. *Star,* Long Island City, July 7, 1876.
21. *New York Daily Tribune,* June 7, 1876.
22. *Letters from Auguste,* Philadelphia, July 14, 1876.
23. *Evening Telegram,* New York, July 29, 1876.
24. John LaFarge, S. J., *The Manner is Ordinary,* New York, 1954.
25. *Letters from Auguste,* Newport, R.I., August 7, 1876.
26. *Ibid.*, August 17, 1876.
27. *Press,* Philadelphia, September 1, 1876.
28. For instance, the museum of the New York Historical Society has one of these statues.
29. *Letters from Auguste,* New York, September 7, 1876.
30. *Irish World,* New York, September 16, 1876.

CHAPTER IV

1. *Letters from Auguste,* Philadelphia, September 24, 1876.
2. *New York Times,* September 29, 1876.
3. *Ibid.*
4. *Ibid.*
5. *Press,* Philadelphia, October 5, 1876.
6. *Ibid.*
7. *Ibid.*
8. *Ibid.*
9. *Letters from Auguste,* New York, October 13, 1876.
10. *Evening Post,* New York, October 20, 1876.
11. *Letters from Auguste,* New York, October 20, 1876.

12. *Boston Daily Globe,* November 13, 1876.
13. *Argus.*
14. *Letters from Auguste,* Newport, R.I., October 30, 1876.
15. *Ibid.*
16. *Ibid.*
17. *Ibid.*
18. Some accounts claim that he married one of his models.
19. *Letters from Auguste,* Montreal, November 3, 1876.
20. MBC.
21. *Letters from Auguste,* New York, November 18, 1876.
22. MBC.
23. *Letters from Auguste,* New York, November 30, 1876.
24. Jeanne to Madame Bartholdi, Newport, R.I., November 30, 1876.
25. MBC.
26. *L'Industriel Alsacien,* Mulhouse, February 14, 1877.
27. *Madame Bartholdi to Auguste,* Colmar, December 22, 1876.
28. Several years later, November 22, 1892, at noon, Bartholdi had his marriage officially confirmed at the city hall of the Sixth *Arrondissement* in Paris. The entry on the marriage register bears the number B 641335 and refers to the actual marriage which took place in 1876. Reverend Brooks is referred to as "minister of the Gospel," followed by Protestant in parentheses. Mrs. Margaret LaFarge's name is given as one of the witnesses. The original marriage document was also signed by Charles B. Marsh, secretary and registrar of the City of Newport, R.I. The reason why Bartholdi had this done is not clear. The transcript obtained by the author from the Parisian city hall says that it was ordered by a judgment . . . rendered by a court on October 28, 1892. By coincidence this was the sixth anniversary of Liberty's unveiling.
29. *Letters from Auguste,* New York, November 27, 1876.
30. *Courrier des Etats-Unis,* New York, January 4, 1877.
31. *Letters from Auguste,* New York, January 8, 1877.
32. *Ibid.,* Albany, January 22, 1877.
33. *Ibid.*
34. Certificate of Award, Sculpture, September 27, 1876, and Centennial Commission Medal, Sculpture.
35. *Exposition Internationale de Philadelphie en 1876, Section Française, Rapport sur les Arts Décoratifs par M. Auguste Bartholdi, membre du jury international,* Paris, 1877, p. 4.
36. *Courrier des Etats-Unis,* February 11, 1877.
37. *Letters from Auguste,* Paris, February 25, 1877.
38. *Ibid.,* August 2, 1877.
39. Jeanne to Madame Bartholdi, Paris, May 24, 1877.
40. *Letters from Auguste,* Paris, November 1, 1877.
41. *Ibid.,* November 7, 1877.
42. Jeanne to Madame Bartholdi, Paris, November 12, 1877.
43. *Letters from Auguste,* Paris, November 15, 1877.
44. "La Tête de la Liberté," *La France,* Paris, October 17, 1878. This article was written by "an engineer."
45. NYPL.

CHAPTER V

1. Charles Lefèbre, "L'Oeuvre de Bartholdi", *Revue Alsacienne*, Paris, 1881.
2. *Ibid.*
3. J. W. Pinchot to Butler, Paris, January 10, 1881.
4. *Ibid.*, Paris, January 20, 1881.
5. *Ibid.*, Paris, April 5, 1881.
6. L. P. Morton to Butler, Paris, December 10, 1881.
7. Bartholdi to Butler, Paris, December 23, 1881.
8. *Letters from Auguste*, Paris, June 9, 1882.
9. *Ibid.*, Paris, June 21, 1882.
10. *Le Petit Journal*, Paris, July 22, 1882.
11. *Ibid.*
12. This organization, for many years under the Presidency of Mr. Albert Halm, has been very active in cultivating among its members the memory of Bartholdi as creator of the Statue of Liberty.
13. *Letters from Auguste*, Paris, August 11, 1882.
14. *Ibid.*, Schinznach, August 14, 1882.
15. *Ibid.*, Paris, October 13, 1882.
16. *Ibid.*, November 22, 1882.
17. *Ibid.*, December 14, 1882.
18. *World*, October 28, 1886. These words in Bartholdi's own handwriting were published as part of the history of the Statue of Liberty.
19. *Letters from Auguste*, December 25, 1882.
20. Rice, *op. cit.*, p. 48.
21. *World*, March 7, 1883.
22. *Ibid.*, March 14, 1883.
23. *Ibid.*
24. *Ibid.*, March 21, 1883.
25. *Ibid.*, May 27, 1883.
26. Ch. Blanc, *Les artistes de mon temps,* Paris, 1876.
27. Louis Giclas, *Album of Light*, Washington, 1924, p. 6, poem by William Tipton Tabott whom Mr. Giclas calls a "local poet."
28. *World*, June 4, 1883.
29. *Ibid.*, June 6, 1883.
30. Quoted by *World*, July 8, 1883.
31. *Ibid.*, September 11, 1883.
32. Information found in *Coney Island News*, June 6, 1885, *Argus*.
33. *Subscriptions to Pedestal for the Statue of Liberty, Prepared by A. S. Sullivan, Esq., member of the General Committee and member of the Bar Committee,* NYHS.
34. *Completion of the Mammoth Statue of Liberty Enlightening the World, Banquet given by Mr. Henry F. Gillig in honor of M. Auguste Bartholdi, the sculptor, Wednesday Evening, May 21, 1884,* p. 8.
35. *Ibid.*, p. 19.
36. *Mouvement Scientifique, Argus.*
37. *Le Siècle*, Paris, July 5, 1884.
38. Rice, *op. cit.*, p. 59.
39. *Le Siècle*, July 5, 1884.
40. *Inauguration of the Statue of Liberty Enlightening the World by the President of the United States,* 1887, p. 7.
41. This plaque was placed there in the course of a ceremony which took place May 23, 1960.

CHAPTER VI

1. *Journal Illustré*, Paris, 1884, undated clippings, Argus.
2. *Le Temps, Paris,* December 1, 1884.
3. Rice, *op. cit.*, p. 5.

4. *Subscriptions to Pedestal for the Statue of Liberty, op. cit.*
5. *Argus,* undated.
6. *Le Temps,* Paris, August 23, 1884.
7. This article was in chapter IV.
8. *New York Times,* undated, *Argus.*
9. The appeal came out in March 1885, and was reprinted by *World* in the October 28, 1886 issue which is quoted here.
10. *World,* March 16, 1885.
11. *Ibid.,* March 19, 1885.
12. *Ibid.,* March 18, 1885.
13. *Ibid.*
14. *Ibid.,* March 20, 1885.
15. Signed "Hard Times," in *World,* March 20, 1885.
16. *World,* March 22, 1885.
17. *Ibid.*
18. *Ibid.,* March 25, 1885.
19. *Ibid.,* March 30, 1885.
20. This name is also found printed as Siddalls.
21. *World,* April 4, 1885.
22. *World,* April 6, 1885.
23. *Ibid.,* April 10, 1885.

CHAPTER VII

1. *World,* April 16, 1885. The contents of this letter had been passed on to the newspaper by Butler.
2. Quoted by *World,* May 3, 1885.
3. *World,* April 22, 1885.
4. *Ibid.,* May 6, 1885.
5. *Ibid.,* May 8, 1885.
6. *Ibid.,* May 12, 1885.
7. This book is referred to in these notes and references as Rice.
8. Rice, *op. cit.* p. 33.
9. *World,* May 12, 1885.
10. *Ibid.,* May 16, 1885.
11. *Ibid.,* May 17, 1885.
12. *Argus,* undated.

13. *Ibid.*
14. *Harper's Weekly,* June 6, 1885.
15. *World,* May 15, 1885.
16. *Ibid.,* August 11, 1885.
17. *Ibid.*
18. *Letters from Auguste,* October 31, 1885.
19. *Argus,* undated.
20. *Ibid.*
21. *Ibid.*
22. *Ibid.*
23. *Ibid.*
24. Charles Butler to Richard Butler, New York, November 21, 1885.
26. *Argus.*

CHAPTER VIII

1. *Chicago Tribune,* September 26, 1886.
2. *Press,* Philadelphia, April 27, 1886.
3. Evarts to Butler, Washington, July 27, 1886.
4. *New York Daily Tribune,* September 26, 1886.
5. *Ibid.*
6. *Ibid.,* October 24, 1886.
7. *World,* October 25, 1886.
8. *New York Herald,* October 26, 1886.
9. Press clipping dated October 26, 1886, NYHS.
10. *World,* October 26, 1886.
11. *Ibid.*
12. *New York Herald,* October 26, 1886.
13. NYHS.
14. *World,* October 29, 1886.
15. *Ibid.*
16. It seems that Bartholdi did not see the final design of the monument. In a letter to Richard Butler, dated Paris, June 30, 1887, the artist mentions an eagle on on the pedestal of the proposed

monument. It so happens that the eagle is not on the pedestal of the Lafayette Monument as it is now, but on the pedestal of the Rochambeau Monument, which is located on another corner of Lafayette Square in Washington, D.C.

17. *Harper's Weekly,* New York, October 27, 1886.
18. *Independent,* New York, October 28, 1886.
19. *World,* October 28, 1886.
20. *Argus,* undated.
21. *Independent,* New York October 28, 1886.
22. Press clippings, dated October 27, 1886, NYHS.
23. *New York Herald,* October 21, 1886.
24. NYHS.
25. *New York Herald,* October 27, 1886.

CHAPTER IX

1. *Evening Post,* New York, October 28, 1886.
2. *Morning Journal,* New York, October 29, 1886.
3. *New York Daily Tribune,* October 29, 1886.
4. *World,* October 29, 1886.
5. *Ibid.*
6. *Ibid.*
7. *Ibid.*
8. *Ibid.*
9. *Ibid.*
10. *Ibid.*
11. *Argus.*
12. NYHS.
13. *New York Daily Tribune,* October 29, 1886.
14. *Ibid.*
15. *Ibid.*

16. *Le Soleil,* Paris. November 9, 1886.
17. *New York Daily Tribune,* October 29, 1886.
18. *Argus.*
19. *Ibid.*
20. *Ibid.*
21. *Ibid.*
22. Duplicates of these pictures are in the *Musée Bartholdi* in Colmar.
23. This author also likes to remember Monsieur Marcel Beley from France, who died recently in Philadelphia. This gentlemen had also contributed his mite to the Statue of Liberty project when he was a child. When an attempt was made to start a subscription for a Bartholdi monument in New York, Monsieur Beley was the first to send in a contribution.

CHAPTER X

1. *Le Courrier des Etats-Unis* is a good source for the history of the Statue of Liberty as seen by the French residents of New York. This author has not been able to locate a whole file of this newspaper, but the copies available have been useful.
2. Jeanne to Madame Bartholdi, New York, November 6, 1886.
3. *Ibid.*
4. *World,* October 30, 1886.
5. *Frank Leslie's Illustrated Newspaper,* October 30, 1886.
6. *Le Monde,* Paris, November 6, 1886.
7. *World,* November 14, 1886.
8. Bartholdi to Butler, Paris, April 2, 1890.
9. Bartholdi to Pulitzer, Colmar, October 13, 1887.

10. *Ibid.*
11. Bartholdi to Butler, Paris, February 18, 1887.
12. *Ibid.*
13. Bartholdi to Butler, Paris, April 21, 1892.
14. *Ibid.*, Paris, November 9, 1894. In the same letter he thanks his friend for 3,000 francs which Butler had sent him through a friend.
15. *World,* October 26, 1886.
16. Bartholdi to Glaenzer, August 3, 1883. *Bibliothèque Municipale,* Colmar.
17. Bartholdi to Butler, Paris, August August 3, 1886.
18. Bartholdi to Butler, Paris, June 7, 1889.
20. The Lafayette Monument in Washington is the work of the sculptors Alexandre Falguière and Antonin Mercier, with Paul Pujol as the architect. The figures were cast in Paris in 1890.
21. Turner to Bartholdi, New York, October 15, 1887.
22. Bartholdi to Pulitzer, Paris, October 15, 1887.
23. Pulitzer to Bartholdi, New York, November 1, 1887.
24. MBC.
25. Turner to Bartholdi, New York, October 31, 1887.
26. Bartholdi to Municipal Council of Paris, September 23, 1888.
27. Bartholdi to Pulitzer, Paris, November 15, 1891.
28. A copy of the poem as well as of the program was given to the author by Professor Francis Wayland of Wagner College, New York. It is among the papers and books which belonged to Markham and were donated to the college.

EPILOGUE

1. L. Hirn to Bartholdi, April 21, 1894.
2. *Le Petit Temps,* Paris, July 31, 1898.
3. *New York Times,* October 4, 1904.
4. *Ibid.,* October 9, 1904.
5. *Discours prononcés le vendredi, 7 octobre, 1904, aux obsèques de F. A. Bartholdi,* 1904.
6. *Ibid.*
7. *Ibid.*

Index

About, Edmond, letter to Bartholdi, 17; articles by, 34; visit to Bartholdi's home in Colmar, 34; reaction to articles, 35; with the French press, 37.

Amateur Minstrel Jubilee, 117.

American Committee on the Statue of Liberty, formation, 57f., announcement of final organization, 60; raising money, 76; subscription booklet, 77f.; report on Pedestal Fund, 84; appeal for Pedestal Fund, 86; appeal to Patriotism, 90; authorizes resumption of stone cutting for Pedestal, 95; resumes work on Pedestal, 116; reception of French delegates, 136; issues tickets for unveiling, 138; souvenir book, 149.

American Museum of Immigration, 32, 157.

Arthur, President Chester A., 81, 126.

Aspinwall, Sumner D., Jr., 96.

Avoiron and Company, 77, 162.

Aztec Society, 142.

Babcock, Samuel, 58, 60.

Baheux de Puysieux, Jeanne-Emilie,' visits Bartholdi in Montreal, 52; visited by Bartholdi in Canada, 53; emotion when she sees Bartholdi again, 55; letter to Madame Bartholdi, 55f.; marries Bartholdi, 56; concern about mother-in-law, 59, 68; trip to America, 123; arrival for unveiling, 131f.; at unveiling, 137; at F. de Lesseps' farewell party, 155; death, 169.

Barbour, H. H., 115.

Bartholdi, Albert, 6.

Bartholdi, Amédée, 149.

Bartholdi, Auguste, birthplace, 1; military uniform, 4; birth, 5; name, 5f.; monogram, 6; first attempts at sculpturing, 8; first trip to Egypt, 9f.; second trip to Egypt, 13; lesson from British officer, 14; at St. Borromeo's Statue, 14; Suez project, 14ff.; marriage project, 17f.; plans travel in U. S., 19f., 23; service in Franco-Prussian War, 20f.; first visit to U. S., 23ff.; first impressions of U. S., 24; people he met on first visit to U. S., 25f.; with LaFarge family, 26; with Senator Sumner, 27; with Henry Long-

fellow, 28; his itinerary through U. S. in 1871, 28f.; impression of the Prairie, 29; with Brigham Young, 30; comments on Americans, 31; return to France, 32; summary of first trip to U. S., 32; dinner with Laboulaye, 33f.; departs for second trip to U. S., 40; stay in Philadelphia 1876, 41f.; at Offenbach supper in New York, 41; acquiring copyright for Statue of Liberty, 44; honored at Philadelphia, 48f.; defends himself against accusers in *Press*, 49f.; praised by *Daily Graphic*, 51; in Canada with Jeanne, 53; replies to Madame Bartholdi concerning Jeanne, 54; marriage, 56; sells fountain, 58; return to France after second visit to U. S., 59; report on American fine arts, 59f.; receiving General Grant, 62; secretary for *Union Franco-Américaine*, 63; lottery campaign, 63; praised by Lefèbre, 66; legal proceedings, 68; his Rouget de Lisle, 68; at Schinznach, 70; honored by Legion of Honor, 70; monument to Diderot, 71; with H. F. Gillig, 78; reference to by Senator Bozérian, 79; receives Victor Hugo, 83; announces dismantling of Statue, 97; publication for Pedestal Fund, 115f.; opinion on colossal statuary, 116; writing about Texas, 117; makes third trip to U. S., 122f.; farewell dinner, 126; arrives on *La Bretagne* for unveiling, 131; inspection of Statue in New York, 133; poem on his honor, 136; honored by New York City, 137; received by Produce Exchange, 137; introduction to President Cleveland, 141; presentations to him, 143f.; unveils the Statue of Liberty, 148; at Delmonico's banquet, 151f.; trip to Niagara Falls, 155; farewell in tears, 157; aspirations for Bedloe's Island expressed, 157; expresses belief in American ingratitude, 159; made Commander in Legion of Honor, 160; lawsuit, 161; personal sacrifices incurred for Statue of Liberty, 161f.; sends power-of-attorney to Butler, 163; monument of Lafayette and Washington, 164ff.; making of monuments, 167; conception of art, 168; death, 168f.; statue of Bartholdi by Louis-Noël, 170.

NOTE * designated elsewhere in index by her usual name: Jeanne.

N.B. This index is not complete. Omissions will be rectified in the next edition.